The Turks of Istanbul

The Turks of Istanbul

SHAMBHU T. MERANI

Macmillan Publishing Co., Inc.

NEW YORK

Collier Macmillan Publishers

LONDON

Copyright © 1980 by Shambhu T. Merani

Macmillan Publishing Co., Inc.
866 Third Avenue, New York, N.Y. 10022
Collier Macmillan Canada, Ltd.

Library of Congress Cataloging in Publication Data

Merani, Shambhu T
    The Turks of Istanbul.

    1. Istanbul—Social life and customs.   2. National
characteristics, Turkish.   I.   Title.
DR726.M47   956.3   80-13192
ISBN 0-02-584330-3

10 9 8 7 6 5 4 3 2 1
Printed in the United States of America

To NICKY,
extraordinary companion

Contents

Preface

I LIVED IN ISTANBUL for five years, while representing the International Labour Office in Turkey, Greece, Cyprus, and Israel. Among other matters, I spent these years in the systematic study of the Turkish way of life, the object of which was to write this book, to share with you what I learned. In this study, you will find analysis and understanding of the Turkish psyche—amusement, enlightenment, inquiry, challenge, awakening, history, and glimpses of the future. There are intriguing questions, too. The style of presentation adopted in this book is an attempt to assist you in understanding the Turks and how they do their business.

While it is impossible to recapitulate all, I have tried to show you what I saw, what I heard, what I thought, felt, imagined, and did—and, above all, what I learned during my long stay in the midst of the Turks and in their own setting.

There were many windows of enlightenment open, inward and out, through which shafts of light entered in many shapes and forms; their brightness varied, but their penetration was deep. One question led to another. One observation showed where more could be made. One line of approach or inquiry was not enough. Other directions had to be pursued. Side views and oblique angles were not to be ignored, as these had unique qualities. In every possible way and every day, everywhere the effort was made to learn, to appreciate, to identify, and to go on and on.

The Turkish character and the Turkish way of life were the twin themes of my study. Through my selection of what to say and how to say it, I have tried to illuminate these themes as they are seen in Istanbul; as Istanbul is a part of Turkey, the study also extends somewhat to the Republic of Turkey, and to its past and present, the twins of time. Each glimpse is meant to reveal and illustrate character—the Turkish character.

This character is a powerful one—independent and erect the Turk stands. He can take a lot in his own way, and his Turkish ways make him stand apart. One must remember the frontiers of the land of Turkey and the lands that have belonged to Turkey in the past. Also remember the seas over which Turkey rules and the waters that touch its shores. Its neighbors are many and its friends some more.

It has been difficult to decide where to begin and where to end. So I decided simply to let you see what I saw and hear what I heard as one thing happened or another followed, true to life. Then, having completed writing about the day-to-day affairs of life, I have tried to take you through the frontiers of life of the Turks and the extended frontiers which matter so much—the present going backward and the past moving forward.

SHAMBHU MERANI

Geneva, Switzerland

Acknowledgments

"The Beads of My Turkish Rosary"

It is said that you must always count your blessings. Let me count mine:

- My colleagues and my friends, each in their unique way, were a complete universe in which I had the great pleasure to live and to work.
- My neighbors—they created for me understanding and appreciation of life in Istanbul.
- The opportunity to be in Istanbul and to be able to go in my way through its past and its present.
- To have lived in Istanbul not too short a time, but not too long a time either.
- To have been at Istanbul and in Turkey at a particularly

critical time, when several things happened and when several other things did not happen which should have happened.

- To have seen the martial law at Istanbul for practically all the years that I was there.
- The student unrest—what a mind-opener it was.
- To be where I was when the Americans began to put pressure on Turkey, and to have observed the situation in which the Americans went their way.
- To have seen the results of American actions to prevent the cultivation of poppies.
- From Istanbul to have been concerned with Turkey, Greece, Cyprus, and Israel and to have been there when each of these countries was involved in armed conflicts.
- To have been at Istanbul when the October 1973 Arab-Israeli war broke out.
- To have walked over the bridge of Bosphorus on the day it was opened by the President of the Republic of Turkey and to have felt the shivers of the trembling bridge as it bore its heavy load of dignitaries.
- To have participated in the Fiftieth Anniversary celebrations of the Republic of Turkey.
- To have seen the Turkish workers go abroad in thousands as guest workers in other countries. And, alas, to see them go no more.
- To have lived where I lived in Istanbul.
- To have made the friends I made there.
- To have had the honor to meet President Cevdet Sunay and then also to have had the pleasure and honor to meet his successor President Fahri Koruturk. It was also a great pleasure to have met the former President and Prime Minister Ismet Inonu, a leader of earlier times.
- To have been there when the President retired and was succeeded by another and to have witnessed the working of the whole process of selection and changeover.

- The opportunity to see political elections in Turkey and also to see political changes; to see how coalition governments are formed and not formed, and how the country is governed when there is no government in power.
- The opportunity to have had meetings with each successive head of government during my five-year stay:

  Prime Minister Suleyman Demirel
  Prime Minister Nihat Erim
  Prime Minister Perit Melen
  Prime Minister Naim Talu
  Prime Minister Bulent Ecevit
  Prime Minister Suleyman Demirel
  Prime Minister Bulent Ecevit
  Prime Minister Suleyman Demirel
  Prime Minister Bulent Ecevit

- Equally, the opportunity to have known and worked with, over and over again, each one, as one succeeded the other, the Ministers and their Undersecretaries, Deputy Secretaries, Assistant Secretaries, and Heads of Departments and their seniormost colleagues concerned with several important subjects. To have been involved, at the policy, planning, and administrative levels, in the consideration of such subjects as employment, migrant workers, rural development, land reform, vocational training, management development, productivity, tourism, youth development, safety and health, cooperatives, family planning, inequalities, research and development, social security, exports, industrial development, industrial relations, wage and collective bargaining, legislation, small-scale industries and handicrafts.
- To have sat in the Parliament to listen to the debates, as an observer.
- The opportunity to have known the Mayor of Istanbul and

his successor, too, not only in his office but also on the dance floor.

- To have known and worked with a large international community at Istanbul and a much larger one at Ankara.
- To have worked in close collaboration with many international organizations, and to have known the representatives of many countries.
- The opportunity to have been closely associated with several field activities.
- It was a blessing indeed to have known the Trade Union Movement in the most comprehensive way possible; its national and regional leadership, its rank and file, and above all to have worked with them in close cooperation on various themes of importance.
- Equally, to have worked closely with the leadership of the Turkish Employers Confederation and its national and regional organizations and with individual employers on a variety of subjects close to their hearts and to my own, too. To have visited many managements and many trade unions at the enterprise level.
- The opportunity to live and to work with the academic community at Istanbul and at Ankara.
- To meet persons of eminence in widely diverse social, economic, planning, industrial, and policy fields. To know various national organizations, national institutes, and voluntary bodies of importance, and to come in close contact with their leaders.
- To have attended and participated in many discussions, meetings, conferences, conventions, congresses, and seminars on many subjects, and to have attended several public meetings.
- The opportunity to meet and discuss with the common man, in almost every walk of life, was great indeed.
- To have been exposed widely and continuously to all that Turkey has to offer, and be able to receive and to absorb the reality of life in the great city of Istanbul.

- To have driven in Istanbul when driving was anarchy, a dare and a scare.
- To do what I did and the life that I lived. To have seen and heard and felt and imagined what now are the "glimpses" of the Istanbul-Turkish psyche.

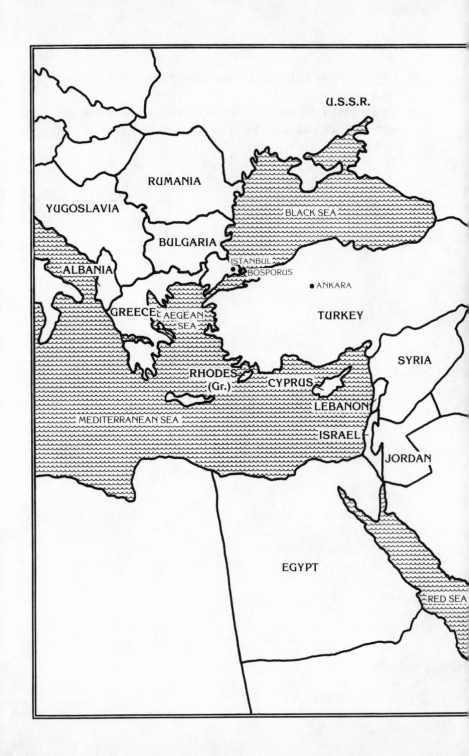

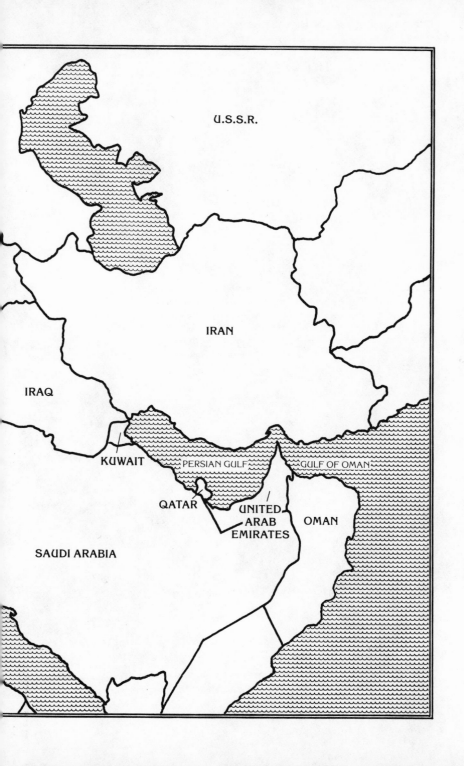

The Turks of Istanbul

1. Istanbul, the City

THE CITY OF BYZANTIUM was founded by Greeks in 667 B.C. In
A.D. 330, Byzantium was rebuilt by the Roman Emperor Constan-
tine I. It was renamed Constantinople and made the capital of the
Roman Empire. The Roman was succeeded by the Byzantine
Empire and Constantinople became its capital. In 1453 the city,
which for eleven centuries had been the capital of the Roman
and Byzantine empires, was conquered by the Turks. After World
War I, although occupied by the Allies, the city remained capital
of the Ottoman Empire until 1923. In 1923 newly built Ankara
became the capital. In 1930 Constantinople became Istanbul.

What a long time Istanbul has taken to become itself!

Rome was built by the Romans on seven hills, and Rome is
called the "Eternal City." While some think that Eternal City is
the name given to Rome because it is the seat of the Pope and
Christianity, there are others who think that the Eternal City is
called eternal for its beauty. Istanbul was also built by Roman

hands and it also stands on seven hills. Istanbul is another Eternal City—because of its eternal beauty! Istanbul is a city of splendor. What a rare identity it has! So glamorous and romantic, a merger of the past and the present, unbeaten by the trotting of time.

Built and rebuilt. Conquered, lost, reconquered, reestablished, and regained. Empire followed empire, sultan followed sultan. But the heartbeat of Istanbul has remained unchanged. The identity remains through each period, each civilization, each culture, century by century. All landmarks remain forever.

In slums, in tall buildings and new areas, around the waters and the seas, everywhere and in every walk of life, the identity of the individual also persists. In Istanbul, each inhabitant (there are 3,100,000 of them) has an identity of his own, besides his National Card of Identity. The individual stands alone, erect, aloof, proud, and upright—the unique magnificence of the Turk.

While Ankara is the capital of the secular state of Turkey, Istanbul is the Seat of Islam in Turkey. What Moslem has not prayed at the Blue Mosque in Istanbul, coming even from distances very far away? Istanbul is thus the religious center of Turkey, and Islam is the religion of about 700 million people in that part of the world.

In Istanbul religions meet, for the city is also the see of the patriarch of the Greek Orthodox Church, of a Latin-rite patriarch of the Roman Catholic Church, and of a patriarch of the Armenian Church.

2. The Turks

I MUST SAY SOMETHING about "who are the Turks." If you want to know about the genes and the historical past, read the history, though I am not sure that with facts you would also not get bias. I learned very little that I can regard as hard facts, but what I learned I will share with you. The rest was all hearsay and guess. But in order to know who the Turks are you must know that when blood is spilled it also gets mixed. And when conquerors become sick or when they are defeated or again when their ambitions change, transfers take place, and over the years the past and the present begin to mix.

Everyone will tell you, asked and unasked, "I am a Turk." When you come to know the scene you will realize that some are more Turkish Turks than others. Only when you have learned to identify the cut, note the professions, watch the performance, and distinguish one personality from another will you also see the Cypriot Turks, the Greek Turks, the Jewish Turks, the Druses, the Armenian Turks, and the other Turks by conversion and by convenience.

I was told on good authority that above a certain rank in the armed services everyone is a Turk. I think this is also generally true of the administrative services. In the case of those who look after religion and its various administrative and other aspects, I believe the same is true.

A rich Turk may or may not be a Turkish Turk. But if he is a rich landlord Turk, the chances are that he would be a Turkish Turk. Should he, however, be an agriculturist or a landless laborer, an artisan or a man given to traditional handicrafts, or a mere fisherman or down-and-out poor, a guess would be permissible that the chances are that he is only a poor Turk (though you might come across Greek Turks in this category, too). In the case of services of different types and levels, enterprises of different kinds and size, and shops and stores, you would have to see the patron and the location and the date of birth of the enterprise, the shop and the store, and decide accordingly.

Anyone who has any restriction placed on marriage (i.e., on whom he or she can marry) and further is in the armed services or belongs to any center of power—for example, administration and politics—is more likely to be a Turkish Turk.

In 1923, by an agreement reached in Lausanne (Switzerland), approximately 1.5 million Greeks living in Turkey were repatriated to Greece, and approximately 800,000 Turks living in Greece and Bulgaria were resettled in Turkey. As a result, large numbers of persons, mostly unskilled peasants, were absorbed into Turkey.

Apart from Turkish Turks and Kurds, there are also Greeks, Armenians, Bulgarians, Circassians, Georgians, Arabs, Jews, Druses, and many more. You must particularly know of Cypriot Turks. Istanbul is the seat of the Ecumenical Patriarch, and there are several groups of Orthodox Christians, Gregorians, Roman Catholics, Protestants, and Spanish-speaking Jews. Almost 99 percent of the Turks are Moslem, mostly of the Sunni branch.

3. Apartment

ISTANBUL IS A WINDY CITY. This is a city where the foreigners live together, mostly. It is a city in which the rich live together beside the rich. It is also a city in which the Turks live by themselves. Where would you like to live in Istanbul? I will tell you where I lived when I came to live there.

Taking my welfare into account and being my well-wishers, my colleagues had made a lot of inquiries and research as to the area in which I should live and even selected some possible localities, villas, and apartment blocks. In this they had been guided by certain important facts, namely, where every foreigner lived (shall live and had lived), where they themselves were living, and even where my many predecessors over the long years had lived. So the first two days after my arrival I made the rounds in their company and in the company of others who had accompanied them on their rounds.

But I put forward my point of view as early as I possibly could: I wanted to live in the midst of the Turks, in their exclusive company. I did not wish to live where the foreigners had lived or with other foreigners. I had come to Turkey to live with the Turks and I was, therefore, looking at what had been selected for me in rather a biased way. More than looking at the area, the location, or the villa, I was looking at the faces of those who were living there and who would become my neighbors.

All my colleagues laughed at me. "You do not know the Turks." "You do not even know Turkish." "You have no previous experience of living in Istanbul." "Why do you think that everybody lives with everybody else of the same class, culture, and breed?" And on and on it went, laughter becoming even a slight ridicule.

So I put a small advertisement in Turkish in a local Turkish newspaper saying that I wanted an apartment without giving any other details or mentioning any limitations, not even the address, just giving my telephone number. Within an hour or two of the advertisement's appearance, there was a telephone call from a Turk saying that he had an apartment to let. "Can I come and see it?" "Yes." "I will be there in the next few minutes." He then gave the address and suggested the way to go there.

I went along with the chauffeur of the car at my disposal. On the way I asked the chauffeur (who knew English) not to say a word on my behalf either in Turkish or in English, not a word. We drove, not a long distance, and then turning in and out, we reached the designated apartment block. Out came the "Man on the Spot" (*kapici*), who had telephoned on behalf of the landlord, so it seemed. Since I did not know a word of Turkish, he lifted his head up and with his pointed finger showed me where the apartment was. Neither his face nor his hand had to be lifted too much because what he was pointing out was an **apartment** on the first floor. Quickly came my negative shake of the head, saying a positive no. But being a clever man (so I found out then and later came to respect more and more), the *kapici* accepted my shake of the head (a positive no from me but a provisional one for him) with a question mark and asked me what then (so I thought).

As the block was a tall building, I lifted my head as high as I could and pointed my finger to the topmost floor. This seemed to impress him and at once he gestured me to follow him. Leaving the chauffeur behind (he had kindly and faithfully refrained from speaking on my behalf), I went where the *kapici* took me. Into the entrance, through the passage, up to the point where the lift could go no more. It was the top floor we had reached, which I then learned was the thirteenth floor. It was love at first sight, and over the years this love matured and blossomed.

The accommodation was what I needed. But that was the least part of it. The apartment was in a block occupied by the Turks and only the Turks. The adjacent block was the same. The blocks around also gave the same impression. I had found what I wanted. If it were not the womb of Istanbul, it was the closest I wanted to be. The scene was fantastic, out of this world. I had a more than 180-degree view of Istanbul, the Bosphorus, even the Bosphorus Bridge. It was like being the overlord of what lay around and beyond. The apartment was not only on the top of the block, but this block was on top of one of Istanbul's seven hills. On the left, there was "The Hampstead Heath of Istanbul." Whatever moved on the Bosphorus would be on view, and the vessels parked on courtesy visits would be close enough to illuminate us with their lights.

Here I would be on top of the city and its winds. Istanbul is another San Francisco, and being here would be like living in San Francisco. (How true this became when the Bosphorus Bridge was completed! With the lights on the Bridge at night, the illusion was complete.)

From this observation tower I would be able to see the skyline of Istanbul, see the domes of the famous mosques, and hear the prayers of the devotees. Looking across the strait, I would see what Asia has to offer Istanbul. This panorama of life and its ways would also yield deep understanding. The valley with its green ups and downs and the blowing winds would bring the smells of nature that still graced Istanbul. I would be able to look at the Bosphorus all the time—would this not be inspiration enough?

The apartment was completely empty: no electricity, no water, no gas. The windows were unwashed. The floors were not polished. Even the doors did not appear to have received the polisher's touch. It seemed the apartment had not yet been made ready for occupation.

With the usual international gesture of the right hand (never do such things with the left hand)—the index finger and some other fingers open, the hand being turned to reveal the palm—I made a gesture inquiring about the rent. The *kapici*, who had seen a lot of life before, understood my inquiry and taking my hand in his own, wrote with his fingers on my blank palm certain figures. This was the monthly rate he had written.

Then he wanted us to descend so that the further conversation could be conducted with the assistance of my chauffeur. This was exactly what I wanted to avoid, since the chauffeur had also shown contempt for my ambition to live solely in the midst of the Turks.

I therefore remained and resumed my gestures, which I had to improvise on the spot. Again calling on my right hand, I moved it to my lips, with the *kapici* watching, moved it back again toward the nearest ear on the face of the *kapici*, and then withdrew it again (all to his amazement), and using my left hand I worked on it with my right hand as if I were dialing digits of a telephone number. There was the smile of understanding: my reward. Once again the *kapici* wrote some digits on the palm of my hand and I memorized these, the telephone number of the landlord who would be the giver of my dream-reality apartment.

We came down and immediately I drove away with the

chauffeur in the limousine, big in its grandeur. A little way farther, I got out of the car and went back, not to the block but to its environment, to survey better the surroundings and what they had to offer. The first thing I was looking for was grounds where we could walk our golden retriever Nicky, in sun and in rain. What I found was adequate for our use, and round the corner was a shop that displayed meat, fruit and vegetables, bread and milk, and sundries. All seemed to be in order for one's daily needs. A pharmacy board was standing erect within a few yards of where I stood. There was also a haircutting salon (coiffure as it is called in Istanbul, as a mark of respect to the French). While driving back I carefully watched the route. It was about eight minutes from my office by car, all bright and clear, free from any congestion whatever at that time of the morning.

This meant my home would be on the crest of the hill called Gayrettepe, and I would pass through the famous Barbaros Bulvari, then to Besiktas, on to Dolma Bahchi Palace and, passing the Stadium, go on to Gumussuyu Caddesi, and thence to my office. From there I could see "the silver water" (of the Bosphorus), as *Gumussuyu* means in Turkish.

That afternoon I went with my wife and son and Nicky, for them to approve my find of the morning. It was a family joy when their admiration was as great as mine. What Istanbul could offer to the seeker!

The following morning I broke the news to my colleagues about what I had found. The landlord was represented by a lawyer, who at my urgent request came over to my office ready with the contract (the usual well-tried-out one-sided contract). He stated the rent and I agreed to it without bargaining. This disappointed not only my colleagues but also the representative of the landlord.

I asked him when I could have the apartment. He said that it would be ready in about two months' time: there was no water, no electricity, no gas, no this and that. The floors had to be polished and the windows cleaned and even some doors painted.

4. Man on the Spot

As THE BANKS wanting to do international business always advertise the presence of their "Man on the Spot," so should be the case of the Istanbul *kapici*, because he is truly the "man on the spot." The *kapici* is not only the "Concierge," "the Keeper of the Door," and the "Hall Porter," but much more.

Every block of apartments has a *kapici*. He is paid a certain amount each month by the tenants. He also gets a summer and a winter uniform, complete with shoes and coat. From time to time he gets a bonus. Every year he gets a raise in salary. The *kapici* gets holidays like other workers. He also has fixed hours of work, lunch breaks, and shifts of duty, but these are flexible. In our case we paid a consolidated rent for the month which included a certain amount for the *kapici*, and the landlord (his agent) paid the sum to the *kapici*. In addition, we, on our volition and because he did so much for us, paid a certain fixed sum directly to him each month.

A *kapici* has to be a man. It could be a man and his brother, a man and his wife, a man and his wife and his brother, or a man and a man. But never a woman, even if the woman has a husband or a brother or a sister. If you think that this is discrimination against women or lack of equal opportunity for women or a breach of human rights or human ethics, standards, and equalities in general, you are entitled to your own opinion, but do not expect anyone in Istanbul or elsewhere in Turkey to agree with you. After all, it is the *Man* on the Spot that the whole subject is about. But then, in actual practice, you will be heartened to find that given the kind of wife the Turkish wife of a Turkish *kapici* is, she is, in fact, a deputy *kapici* most of the time, doing many jobs to assist him; on other occasions she represents the *kapici*. When she is not helping him, she is busy raising their family.

The *kapici* is an institution. Once appointed, he is generally never removed, so I was told. But as he is above all a person, I will go from the general to the personal and tell you all I can about our *kapici*. As a matter of fact, we had two *kapici* who were brothers.

The younger brother had just married and while we were there his first baby daughter was born. He had taken a separate small apartment for his family in a cheaper area in the city. While doing his military service he had been a parachutist. His father and mother were living in a village near Ankara. Being knowledgeable and enterprising, he had saved and now owned an apartment in the cheaper part of the city which he let out on rent. He had a younger brother for whom he had found a job, through a friend of mine, in a car manufacturing company. Later he moved him to work in a diplomatic mission.

The senior brother had been a soldier in the army. He was married but his wife was at Ankara. He had a son who was a soldier in the army, posted at Ankara.

The *kapici* looks after the block, the entire premises, the tenants, and is the representative of the landlord. In many ways he is also the custodian. He hands over the premises to you when you rent them and gives you the key. When you leave you hand the key back to him and he takes over the apartment on behalf of the landlord, examining and counting and noting whatever needs further scrutiny by the landlord or his representative notary. He is your link with the landlord.

If you have any problem that requires the landlord's attention, you tell the *kapici*. He will pass it on and act on the landlord's orders. He will tell you what the landlord has decided to do or not to do. But what the *kapici* says to the landlord will on many occasions determine what the landlord says to the *kapici*, and what will or will not get done. What the landlord cannot do, the *kapici* can accomplish on his own—within limits, but if it is at your expense, with no limit at all.

The *kapici* lives on the premises. The two brothers had a room in the basement next to the hot-water pipes and the central heating apparatus, with all the valves and gauges. A small inner room with a wash basin was attached. When the younger *kapici* stayed with his wife overnight (this happened from time to time before the baby was born), the wife shared the inner room with him. One more thing must be mentioned about this room: whenever the outer entrance door opened or shut, it gave a small ring, which was heard in the *kapici* room. This informed him of the outer gate situation when he himself was not at the gate (though I have a feeling that he would have, during the critical hours of sleep, switched off the mechanism).

The *kapici*'s day began early, very early indeed. Before anyone left in the morning, the *kapici* was there, up and doing. He was up even before the newspaper arrived.

First he surveyed his territory—the entrance to the block and the outside.

Then the *kapici* would sweep the entrance, soap it, wash it, mop it, hand-dry it. He would do the same for the marble steps on the outside. From time to time he washed and cleaned the apron outside the block, and in summer he sprinkled water over the earth that greeted you as you came in (later the earth was replaced by a cement floor). The front space beyond the apron was also of earth. This, too, he cleaned from time to time as it was the car park. (Again, after some years, the car park was cemented from end to end.) The outer gate door was a large one with a lot of brass. This he polished from time to time, and the shine extended to everything of brass (including the lifts). The steps of the thirteen floors were also cleaned by him from time to time, and when the marble steps that extended up to the first floor were soaped and washed, they looked very attractive indeed.

If there were any boxes or litter or any bottles or cartons left outside the apartment door by the tenants, these too were picked away by the *kapici*—who, I am sure, was able to sell them to the *eskici*. The call of the buyers of anything old (*eskicii*) was quite a welcoming sound, and the *kapici* always responded to it.

Apart from cleaning the outside and inside of the lifts, the role of the *kapici* insofar as the lifts were concerned was very important indeed. If the lift got stuck while you were in it, he was the one who bailed you out. This happened frequently, so I will tell you of the first time it happened, during the first three or four days after our being in the apartment.

My wife was in the lift together with our Golden Retriever Nicky. The lift stopped en route to the thirteenth floor as lights went out. My wife rang the emergency bell, though she could not tell whether anyone had heard it outside. It was dark inside, it was summer and hot, and between the two of them they had little air supply. When you are caught and anxious and in unusual circumstances, your breathing gets faster and faster.

Hearing no action (though action was proceeding), she began to thump on the wall of the lift. This she kept on doing, first slowly and infrequently and then continuously. This pounding fetched a response, and neighbors began appearing at different floors. Some then identified where the lift had got stuck. They converged close to the point where the lift stood motionless. Some verbal communication followed and then they knew who had got stuck in the lift (at the time my wife did not speak even one work of Turkish). Shouts began to ring out for the *kapici*. But the remedial action had already commenced.

When he heard the emergency bell, the *kapici* began his climb up the thirteen floors. On reaching the top he had begun the further climb across the boiler-room type of ladder, as in a ship, to reach the loft where the winch of the lift was. When he reached this point (breathless he must have been without doubt, and this was a situation when breath was needed the most), he began single-handedly to pull the lift by its cable. He was in utter darkness, since on this occasion all lights had gone out. He pulled and pulled until the lift moved, and then he pulled more and more, but with less and less speed. Finally the lift reached the thirteenth floor and my wife and my dog could be retrieved.

There was gladness all around and many thanks were expressed to the *kapici* and to the several neighbors who had collaborated in this process. In a way, this opened the gates to many hearts, as many ladies stayed on with my wife that evening to tell her of their experiences and what to expect in future and how to do it the next time. As a result, my wife always carried in her pockets a torch and a whistle.

When I returned from the office late in the evening and heard of this experience, I proceeded to take action to make certain that the lift would not fail again. Action I did take, indeed, but that did not mean that the lift did not again fail many times. It failed when the lights went off, but worse still it failed because it was not maintained well. The repairs were delayed or poorly done. Missing parts were not replaced or the substitutes were not good. But worst of all, the maintenance man did not come when wanted, when he should have come as required by the emergency situation and by the regulations for emergency action.

Since the lift failures occurred at odd hours and affected a lot of tenants, I think everyone decided, subconsciously perhaps, to pay more attention to the comings and goings of the lift. Whenever the lift stopped not at the floor level, neighbors always rushed out. This helped a lot. The greater alertness of the *kapici* also helped a great deal.

I will now return to the *kapici*, although the lift, for those who live on top floors of apartment blocks, is an important matter, and the *kapici* and the lift were much involved with each other.

When you came down in the morning, the *kapici* was generally there to greet you with *Gunaydin* ("Good Morning") and to the door for you. At night it would be *Iyiaksamlar* ("Good Night") if you were returning home. Generally he went to his room at 9:00 P.M. in winter and 10:00 P.M. in summer and, therefore, you opened the door with your key after these hours. If he was there he would see you into the lift or out of it. If you arrived with parcels, he would help you with them from the car to the lift; if they were large or heavy he would help you to your apartment.

In this way he was very helpful to ladies, elderly gentlemen, and children. While he performed the duties of the official doorkeeper, he was not merely a doorman.

There were few green plants outside the apron, but they were his contribution, and it was he who watered them. No stranger could pass by without his knowledge or permission. He looked after the house telephone, and the internal telephone worked only with his assistance and approval. If a distinguished or unknown visitor came, the *kapici* accompanied him to your apartment. The *kapici* knew all the friends, the relatives, the visitors, the persons who received mail. When the postman came, he gave the mail to the *kapici* and they usually had a chat. Later, the *kapici* put the mail into your letter box (the letter box had no name on it and he alone knew which letter to put into which box).

If you wished, the *kapici* washed your car. Of course, you paid him for it at a fixed rate. You could make a regular arrangement —once a day, once every three days, once a week. Any repair you wanted done, you asked him. He did it and you gave him a small tip (*bahsis*). If you had to send a message or a letter, you gave it to him. When you had forgotten to get the bread or some vegetable or any other odd item—or the item was not odd but the time was—he would gladly fetch it for you. No vendors could come into the area without his permission, and each time the *kapici* had to authorize their entry. If you required a taxi, he called one for you, fixing the rate.

In our case, we were afraid of stray dogs, and when they were around he chased them away from us. He looked after the children who played outside the apartments of the block and watched boys and girls come and go. If it became a matter of discipline, he was the first to notice the need and to enforce it. Everyone stopped and talked to him. He knew them all. He had seen births and deaths, courting, *nishan* (engagement), and *nikah* (wedding) of many who lived there. He had seen seniors retire from work. He had seen others complete their studies and sit unemployed.

The police and he knew each other well and he kept them well informed. Matters of security were his special concern. Hence, his visits from time to time to the Security Department. This leads me to mention a special situation. During the peak martial-law situation, the administrator of the martial law had installed for my protection a twenty-four-hour armed guard. This the *kapici* did not like. It was, he thought, a reflection upon him. Did he not look after me well enough? (Which indeed he did.) So, the duty officer and he came to an arrangement: the duty officer was for appearance, the real protection, such as was needed, was the sole concern of the *kapici*.

In any emergency, day or night, the *kapici* was the first person to become involved. If there was no water in your apartment—this happened on several occasions—the *kapici* brought up buckets of water or filled them for you to carry upstairs. The central heating was also his concern—when to put it on, at what temperature to keep it, to reduce the temperature every night, and then finally when to shut down. It was the *kapici* who came to see if the radiators were working or were warm enough.

The *kapici* raised the Turkish flag on festival, religious, and national days. On one occasion he elected to show the flag from our apartment window so that it could fly as high as the heavens would allow.

The *kapici* was the eyes and and ears of everyone, especially of those who mattered. But he never gossiped or spoke ill of anyone (to my knowledge). What a capacity he had to get on with one and all, young and old, men and women, high and low.

Dogs are unwelcome in Turkey. This made a problem for our *kapici* (the younger brother.) He saw that we loved Nicky infinitely more than he had ever seen such love before shown to someone other than one's own child. He saw us kiss him, hug him, and purchase excellent meat for him every day. He knew that Nicky slept in our bedroom and during the day the salon was his, where he would sit on the sofa and listen to music. He could not for a long while understand this. Gradually, he began to see our point of view and then, would you believe it, when no one was around or was ever to see him do it, he would quietly embrace our dog, give him a hug and a kiss. As time passed, the *kapici* grew bolder; he would call Nicky by sweet names, speak to him, even let him cross the floor when the floor was wet and specially arrange for him to go up by the lift whenever it was possible.

The *kapici* never made any request. But we became such friends that he would bring from his village wheat flour hand ground (and refused to accept any money for it). When I brought him tea from my visits to India, it was a gift to a friend. If you gave him, on occasion, some clothes or shoes or meals or sweets or flowers, this too you did as you would give to someone close to you. When my son visited me, the *kapici* always give him a small present on arrival and on leaving. If he found you were wearing something new, special, or to his liking, he would wish you *gule, gule* ("May you enjoy it"). On holidays, festival days, and Moslem prayer days, it was quite common to see some neighbor give him a meal of lavish size and variety, for lunch or for dinner.

When we had a reception or a dinner, he helped us as a bearer. Sometimes he brought his youngest brother, too, and between the two of them we never had to seek further outside help. Then, naturally, after the guests had left, we gave him whatever he liked of the remains for himself.

He got us a live-in maid at our request, but being a moralist, when he found that she was flirting with the martial-law duty officer, he told us so and on his own shooed her off. On another occasion we got a live-in boy, obtained with the help of a colleague. The *kapici* did not like this (we had asked him to find us one, but he had not succeeded), and soon he sent the boy away on the grounds that he had found him smoking. Again, a moralist, a guardian, and a custodian. Of course, he helped us to get a weekly cleaning woman and, as one left, he got us another.

The *kapici* had a link with the *kapici* of the next block, and between them Block A and Block B were fully covered. The *kapicii* have a trade union of their own.

The *kapici* helps the landlord to find a tenant. He helps anyone who needs an apartment to find one. In this way he is an estate agent. The *kapici* was the one who implemented the decisions of the Board of Management of the block under the authority of the director appointed by the board.

The *kapici* gave you such help and affection that you always felt him as your equal. How he was so much to each tenant and how he could work so hard were his secrets.

---

5. Neighbors

I WANT TO TELL YOU ABOUT MY NEIGHBORS: thirty-nine in the block in which I lived, forty in the adjoining block, and some more across the street. Although I came to know almost every one of them, I will introduce those who were special in some ways, some who represented the type, some others from whom I learned this or that, some who illustrate the points I am making, and those who became good friends whom I will always cherish.

My apartment was an observation tower from which I could be in contact with my neighbors of Block B, in which I lived, Block A, which was adjacent, and then a large number of blocks in the front, to the left and to the right, ahead and beyond, with the entire apartment complex in which I lived containing about 2,000 to 3,000 modern Turkish families, educated, sophisticated, and well paid. Some rich ones, too. In Istanbul, what greater area of observation could one ask!

First, about my landlord (in Istanbul, the landlord is called Lord of the Apartment). He was a bachelor and belonged to the Diplomatic Service at Ankara; on my first visit to the capital I called on him. A few months later when he came to Istanbul (his sister was living in the same block), he visited us. He was then

transferred to an Eastern European country and on the completion of his tour of duty, he finally returned to settle down in
Istanbul in his own apartment. He was very upset because he had
to go through many difficulties, although he was living next to his
sister in a separate apartment. He wanted me to leave my apartment, and one of the strongest arguments that won him my sympathy was the fact that he argued over and over again that he was
a bachelor and, therefore, alone. (He, with his housekeeper of
long standing, indeed made a very lonely pair!)

On the thirteenth floor my immediate neighbor, who had so
kindly taken to us on the day of our arrival and thereafter, was
a schoolteacher (she retired while we were there), whose husband
belonged to the secret service (he too retired while we were on
the scene). Neither of them spoke English, but their daughter,
who had married a few days before we moved in, spoke English
well and was a secretary with the leading holding company in
Turkey. Soon the daughter and her husband left for the United
States. The son of the house did his army service and we saw
him go in and out. He spoke English and had been working as
a freelance tourist guide. He met a Swedish girl (formerly a nurse)
and they got married. Then, in due course, they had a daughter.
Equally in due course, the wife, after going back and forth
between Sweden and Turkey, even doing some teaching of children at Istanbul, returned to her own home country. The son took
up a ready-made clothing business, and with the help of his retired
father and mother serviced the needs of Sweden and Germany by
selling what could be sold because it was the cheapest. The wife
resumed hospital nursing in Sweden.

Through her understanding and her friendship, our neighbor
gave us a great deal for hardly any comparable return we could
possibly make. She taught my wife the Turkish language, Turkish
cuisine, Turkish habits, Turkish ways, even some Turkish slang.
Often she brought Turkish coffee to our apartment to drink it
with us. Some time after we left she too left and went to live
elsewhere, although the apartment was her own.

The third apartment on our floor remained without an occupant for nearly one and a half years. No one would take it, as everyone knew all about the thirteenth floor and what it represents in life. The lord of the apartment was a Bulgarian. He gave the greatest publicity to the fact that an English-speaking foreigner was now living on the thirteenth floor, that he was a diplomat, that many friends from many foreign countries were visiting him frequently, and that he had Turkish friends almost everywhere who were coming to him freely and in large numbers. This was done so as to improve the acceptability of the block to the foreigners (and his apartment in particular, as this was the one on our floor). In his process, we also learned that no foreigner had yet lived in this or in any similar block. At last, a junior member of U.S. armed forces arrived with his American wife. They did not last too long, because (as the report in the block went) he had quarreled with a Turk and had therefore to be withdrawn. Some months went by with the apartment unoccupied.

Then came another American, Hungarian by birth, also a member of the American armed forces, fresh from Vietnam, with his German wife and three lovely children. She was a wonderful friend and an excellent neighbor, and we missed them when they left two years later on transfer to Germany. The vacancy arose again, but by this time water flowed, the lift moved, and no one had yet died or been spirited away, so the fear of the unlucky thirteen grew less and less. Within the next few months a newly married businessman arrived to live with his wife, with daily visits from the mother-in-law and the father-in-law. Even before you could count nine and nine, the baby arrived and the family lived happily thereafter. The wife used to come to us to telephone her parents, friends, and the doctor (since the baby, being born too early, always needed one). She spoke only Turkish, while her husband spoke the English which is commonly heard in Turkish shops. He was a decorator and a Turkish Jew.

Another neighbor was a retired pilot from the Turkish Air Force and he lived with his wife, one sister, one grown-up son, and one daughter. Soon one sister married and left. Then she used to visit him with her small baby. The daughter married too while we were there. The son was at the university with no intention of competing his studies, which, incidentally, kept the military service away. He spoke English (his father too spoke some limited English with a heavy accent) and we became excellent friends. In his company I saw almost all of Istanbul, even more than the naked eye could see. We went to concerts, pictures, operas, madrigals, shops, streets, lanes and by-lanes. From time to time he had worked as a tourist guide.

The father was working as a night shift manager far out of Istanbul, but this job lasted just a few weeks after our arrival, so he was always at home. The family had a summer house and the father and his wife went by a Turkish coach to Europe on a trip of their dreams. Eventually, the son too got married.

Another neighbor was a lawyer. Neither he nor his charming wife spoke any English, but he spoke Bulgarian, Rumanian, and Russian and some words of German. One day he explained that it was a pity that we did not speak any of his languages; but when my wife learned Turkish, they became quite close to us. His parents had come from Bulgaria and, therefore, he was a Bulgarian Turk. He owned his apartment. As they had no children of their own, the young daughter of the wife's sister came to be with them all the time.

Another neighbor had retired from the armed forces. He had a wife, two daughters, and a son. The eldest daughter was working in a bank. The second one was working in a sales office of an auto company. The son had finished military service and thereafter, having returned an altered person, neither did any job nor spoke to anyone. No member of the family spoke any English, but the second daughter went to the U.S. on a visit to her aunt and came back with a few words of English. The father was very worried that his daughters were still unmarried. He was a deeply religious man.

Because of the initiative of the Bulgarian lord of the apartment, a Bulgarian did ultimately materialize, but he came to live on a lower floor. He had a wife and two sons. None of them spoke any English. While he spoke Turkish extremely well, neither his wife nor his sons could speak any Turkish. He was the consul who issued visas to outgoing Turks. He spoke not a word to anyone, not even a smile. One knew, though, when he was passing because instead of his voice, one always heard the squeaking of his shoes. When the time came to leave Istanbul by car and I knew that I would have to pass through Bulgaria, I caught him by his sleeve one day and inquired about the visa possibilities. He said that I should send the passport to his office and the needful would be done on the spot. When the passport went to him the next day, the needful was done in this sense: as no visa whatever was required by me, it was not necessary to do anything at all.

One neighbor was a noble lady; she was noble by birth, noble by marriage, and noble by profession. In her years, she had grown with her wealth and helped it to grow more and more. She looked after her assets of land, real estate, and mining interests with great skill and success. Between herself and her well-groomed and well-appointed son, she owned and shared three or more apartments and had some others too to spare and rent, all in the block in which we lived. She had a twinkle in her eyes, a smile on her lips, and a touch of humor in whatever she said and did. Her daughter had been married to the son of a former president who was also a former prime minister of the Republic of Turkey, whom I had the honor to meet at Ankara when he came out of deep retirement to address a trade union convention at which I was a guest. As this lady, my dear neighbor, was the sister of my landlord and looked after his apartment while he was away, we came to know each other well and became good friends.

I also became a good friend of her son, whose business interests were wide enough to cover new friends too (he was, during the last part of our stay, working on the sales side with a large auto manufacturing company in Istanbul). The son was married and had two children and was living next to his mother. The mining interests led them to obtain the collaboration of some West German institutions, which in turn sent out a senior representative to stay close to the family and look after the interdependent mining interests. This representative also lived in the block next to the family with his wife and a young daughter. Both were Germans and both became our very good friends. So we came to know more of their individual and joint business interests and different approaches. Soon after our settling down, the noble lady and her son and the son's wife invited us for dinner and we enjoyed for the first time the warm Turkish hospitality.

Another neighbor was a schoolteacher, divorced, attractive, though not young, living with her grown-up daughter. Because her daughter spoke a few words of English we got together from time to time. The mother owned the apartment in which they lived and seemed to belong to the class of the well-to-do. In due course, the son of my pilot neighbor with whom I saw a good deal of Istanbul and who explained to me a great deal too about student life, unrest, employment, careers, marriage requirements, and the rest of it, eventually acted on his own understanding of life and married the daughter. And what he wanted from his marriage partner, he got in his lap, just a few floors below: a girl who would look after his home, give him children (a son to begin with), who was the sole heir of her wealthy mother, who could hold a job, and who would find it difficult to change partners. A true example of "Practice what you preach," "Boy meets girl," and "What are you looking for"!

I learned a great deal from one particular neighbor, and as he had much to offer for observation and study, it would seem an advantage to introduce him in some detail. I was there in close contact with him and his family for most of my days at Istanbul. I hope this profile in depth will aid understanding of those who practice Islam. It will also show in some detail the building up and the working of a Turkish family.

As he knew some broken English and lived on the first floor, I came into touch with him. He offered almost a complete universe for study. With passage of time his English improved, as did my understanding of Turkish. He also made use of the English and Turkish dictionaries frequently, and some books of general information.

He was the one who had helped me with the electrical and the gas connections which I was able to obtain by accompanying him to the authorities concerned. He was always ready to help. He went with me to the lift engineer one night. When there was an epidemic of cholera he helped several neighbors, even from distant blocks, by taking them for inoculation. He was always available, having retired from the business of making and selling Turkish helva and other sweets.

He was a landlord, owning the apartment in which he lived and the next apartment, which he let out on rent (there was a rapid turnover among his tenants, and his apartment used to lie vacant for long periods of time). His sister had two apartments in the adjacent block. He had some land elsewhere, too.

He was, therefore, neither self-employed nor employed by anyone, though once when he traveled frequently he said that his tours were connected with the sale of washing machines (he did not of course expect you to believe this story). He said that he was a journalist of some kind, though nothing appeared over his signature. Every morning he used to get the most rightist daily newspaper, and some neighbors thought that he worked for it.

Usually he was silent and minded his business. From time to time he remained indoors, invisible, unheard from, for ten to fifteen days at a time.

He had a station wagon that he repaired himself, with the help of his family. It was put to many uses. He had equipped it with all repair gear, tents, accessories, and spare parts. He often met with road accidents. From time to time he went out and came back with bulk purchases of vegetables, fruits, and other edibles. He went with his children to fetch water for drinking in large glass jars from special places well known for drinking water.

Three times while we were there he went to Mecca, taking

with him a group of journalists (each paid a share and a little more). He had organized these trips most economically and effectively and himself drove nonstop for unbelievable stretches of time. He came back richer. He even brought back some precious stones and other gems to sell in Istanbul—so he said. He practiced Islam fully and effectively: prayers at home; prayers at the mosque; prayers at Mecca; reading of the Koran all the time; discussing Islam; spreading Islam. Every member of his family, particularly his children, were brought up in the rigid theory and practice of Islam.

He believed that Turkey was not going in the right direction. Turkey's future lay with other Islamic countries and not in being either alone or with the European Economic Community (EEC). He was not in favor of Western ways. He was unhappy at what the Freemasons and the Jews had done and were continuing to do to Turkey. He could not bring himself to believe how my native country (India) could have steel plants. He used to have long discussions with my wife about the fate of Moslems in my country and continued to believe that Moslems were oppressed everywhere except in completely Moslem countries. He wanted to leave Turkey if Turkey did not go the religious way; he would go over to Saudi Arabia, the only truly Islamic country and a country with a future, he felt.

He used to play an active role in the management of the apartment blocks. He was most careful with accounting matters and always spent several days at bookkeeping and management of bank statements to complete his income-tax affairs. He knew the legal system in Turkey well. He was always awake and aware, day and night, and nothing passed or happened without his head popping out of his window to take a full look. In this activity his wife always joined him, and when he was not at home, his wife did it alone.

He never asked anyone for anything. He was always polite and courteous and his gestures were truly Islamic. He and his whole family observed Ramadan fast for the whole month. He performed all religious duties most religiously—his sons' circumcision and the shaving of his sons' heads at appropriate intervals. He always wore a prayer garment and a prayer cap while at home. He was always standing (even when sitting) erect, alone (except with his family), aloof, upright.

He had almost unlimited physical capacity and stamina, and he and his family were well fed and well looked after. He devoted several hours every day without fail to the education of each of his children (his children also devoted several hours to study, including the instruction of those who were younger than they). He was most strict in the enforcement of moral standards, and each one in his family was trained in the practice of Moslem ethics. He had a plan for the career of each of his children and took the greatest interest and care in the development of these plans. Each of his children was at the top of the class and none of them ever failed in any subject. So careful was the homework!

He was a person who practiced what he preached—the teachings of his religion. What he had set up and continued was not just a joint family, not an arrangement in which each one felt secure and wanted and important and loved, but a total system, a way of life, the Turkish way of life.

He took his entire family in his station wagon, twice a year, for long holidays during the vacation period of the schools. This gave them rural life, sunshine, and swimming. It taught them to do things together, each one helping the other, managing affairs without the conveniences of their apartment, looking after their very old grandmother, and a not-too-young sister. These opportunities were also most welcome to the lady of the house, who otherwise carried family responsibilities from the kitchen to the bedroom.

When his eldest son turned fourteen, he taught him how to drive the station wagon. Then the eldest son taught the next one how to drive. By this time the sister was also ready to learn. This left only the last two sons, who were eagerly helping the others in doing odd jobs on the family wagon while biding their time until they could learn to drive too. None of them of course had a driving license.

There was total and instant obedience and love shown to the father, the mother, the grandmother, and the elderly widowed sister. The interdependence of each one on the other was complete. All was within the family—the pleasure and the pain. The grandmother was taken for a walk or from one apartment to the other, three times a day, by different children, under the protective look of the father and the mother. The grandmother and the sister were an integral part of the most integrated circle.

The relations among the children were excellent. Their relations with other boys and girls of the same age, a younger age, and their seniors were also excellent. They with their equals all went to their respective schools together and came back together. They all knew how to cycle. The youngest son, who had just been born as we arrived, grew faster than most, grew almost every day, and grew on his own too, with just a little support from his father and mother, a little hand from his brothers and sisters. Though they could afford it, they never ever had any help for the youngest. The family never engaged any outside help even for the heaviest of work. The equality in the home was complete between the children. The mother, the grandmother, the elderly sister, and of course the father were the most equal ones.

Each one knew how to work, work hard, work with hands (as they grew up they also learned how to use their heads). The togetherness of the family was a happy sight. It was a total family, not just a joint one. The social role played within the family and outside the family was something to admire.

As a neighbor, you could not desire more than he. As a citizen, he was most critical of the manner in which the city and the state were run and in total disagreement with the political structure and the government both in power and out of power. He was most critical of external assistance, influence, pressure, temptations. In his home he was a leader, a teacher, a commander, a preacher, a father, a friend, a guide, an instructor, a taskmaster, a holder of hands. He did not rule by rod, but by love. He was sometimes harsh, but not a tyrant or a dictator. He did not live by love alone either.

The lady of the house was somewhat younger than her husband but in excellent health in spite of having raised a family of five children. She was in complete command of her home, a full partner of her husband. She was also religious and pious. She kept the kitchen and the home and usually stayed inside her home. She had no need to come out to buy from the callers and the criers, as there was always the husband or one of her children present to do her commands and her errands. She looked after the mother-in-law and the elderly sister-in-law, and although they between themselves had two apartments, the apartments were nevertheless part of one system. She did not ask for any outside help at any time, not even for the polishing of shoes. Her own parents were living in a rural suburb, some thirty kilometers away, and that is where her whole family went for long, short, and sometimes weekend holidays. She was content and happy and master of herself.

The eldest son was a bright person and ready to do and to learn whatever his father proposed. He had grown up tall and had made progress in all directions except that he had not had friends from other neighborhoods and did not spend enough time playing with others. He also actively assisted his sister and brothers in learning and doing various things, including a hand in dealing with schoolwork and other home duties. As years passed, he became a companion to his father, too.

The daughter, the only one, was modest, bright, first in her class, devoted to two or three girlfriends. Sometimes the father would drive her to her school when she grew up and on these occasions her two girlfriends also traveled with her. She loved everyone in her home and outside too. Unfortunately, her health was not good and she developed a lung problem. This was a shadow cast over the entire family and the greatest care was taken by everyone to get her back to good health. She too learned driving. She was brought up in strict Moslem religious order and her dresses and hairstyle were extremely sober.

Then there was the second son. He had two ideals to follow: his father and his elder brother. He was almost always with one of them. His studies were carefully supervised. There were two sons younger than he. The youngest son of the family was jumping levels month by month and soon he was even riding a bicycle. He also used to have his head shaved religiously each summer.

The father's mother was most carefully and lovingly looked after, and there was always some boy or girl leading her by the hand, either going upstairs or downstairs. The father, his wife, the father's sister, and each of the children used to keep the grandmother well informed and surrounded by love and their company. She was not unwell for a single day during our long stay.

The elderly sister of the father, widowed or separated, ran a tailoring establishment to which she went in the morning and returned in the evening. Her dress was always the same, extremely sober and neat and clean. She was not attractive but in perfect order, able to look after herself except that her income-tax, legal, and marital matters were the charge of her brother.

The family lived an inner life of their own, in close proximity, in total contact all the time, spending days and nights in the true faith of Islam. Complete fulfillment in a total way of life. How marvelous it was to see the individual as a part of a whole and the whole belonging to each individual who made it!

Well before I left, all other foreigners had left. The Americans had gone home, the Germans had no more gains to make, and the French had found their match. When I left, there was still one hangover from the past. He was the Bulgarian consul who was needed to provide visas when visas were needed. What a turnover of occupiers, owners, and landlords had taken place within so short a time in the life of Istanbul!

Now a little about the neighborhood. Apparently, there was little sickness in any home because doctors rarely came and the sick never went elsewhere. There were few bachelors in the block in the sense that few men were living on their own. Some ladies lived alone, but they had been with men before. Three times the massive glass of the heavy outer entrance door was smashed: once by the force of wind and twice by the vanity of man who cared not what stood, mere glass, between him and where he wanted to be.

All classes, types, men, women, children, of different levels, shapes, and forms, born and bred here or elsewhere, doing this or that, lived in the block with different years of vintage to their credit—the married, the divorced, the separated, the hopefuls, but none poor and deserted. Some owned what they had. Others owned elsewhere while they lived on what they earned. All were educated and self-reliant. There were some with a past, others with a future ahead, though most were on the middle of the road. They lived in harmony, peace, and accommodation.

6. 'Round the Corner

As THERE IS ALWAYS SOMETHING 'round the corner, I must tell you about what is 'round the corner in Istanbul. He is the *bakkal.*

He is the shop 'round the corner—a grocer, an *epicier*, a *petit marché*, a butcher, a wine shop, seller of bread, butter, and cheese, a fruit seller, a vegetable vendor, a *mercerie*, a store, and much more. He is an institution. And there is one for every three or four large blocks of apartments. Some new blocks have one each.

To make him appear in all his glory and dimension I will tell you about my *bakkal*. Immediately after our arrival at the apartment, I went and made his acquaintance on the recommendation of the *kapici*, who told me which one to see.

The *bakkal* gave us a warm welcome ("*Hos geldin*") and with a smile greeted us with "*merhaba.*" With these two words and with his smile we became friends, a friendship that continued throughout our stay. We told him what our immediate needs were and these he sent to our apartment with his young assistant.

The *bakkal* had three rooms. One had the main supplies. You name it and he had it, except medicines, which were in the next-door pharmacy. Bread, milk, yogurt, jams, cheeses, spices, salami, matches, candles, school notebooks, some playthings, everything that a home needs. In the second room he had cold drinks, wines, liquors, beer, bottled water, vegetables, fruit, and the necessary groceries. In the third room the butcher had whatever you required cut to your taste.

The patron and his senior colleague made up the management, and two young boy assistants made the round of the apartments two, three, and even four times a day. Of course there was a small cash register, to do the additions and the subtractions, though no payment receipts were made out. You should never ask a Turk to do arithmetic or any clerical work.

The *bakkal* has a telephone used like a public telephone by many customers, as many homes do not have a telephone. The *bakkal* also receives messages for you over the telephone and sends out his assistant to let you know when there is a call for you.

First thing in the morning, he sends to your apartment the daily Turkish newspaper if you have given him a standing order. Then the young assistant comes around to ask you what you want for the morning, the midday, the whole day, as you wish. He has a notebook in which he briefly scribbles your commission. This way he covers some floors of the block. Another assistant would be doing the same for other floors.

When fresh bread arrives (twice a day) and the supplies of milk and yogurt and *ayran* (yogurt with water), fresh vegetables, and fruit and meat have all come in, the boy assistant fills his basket and brings to you all you ordered. This protocol is repeated in the afternoon. You have what you want, fresh, twice a day, delivered to you at your doorstep. Bread is generally in a separate basket and still hot when it is brought to you. You can select the one you want, half of it too, if you wish. It is not only a home-delivery service or door-to-door service. It is a highly personalized service to meet individual requirements of almost every household need, and sometimes personal need.

At the end of the day (the second round) you paid for what you had received. Some paid at the end of every week or every month. The *bakkal* did as you wished.

---

7. Callers and Criers

LIVING IN A MODERN BLOCK OF APARTMENTS in a new housing complex, with neighbors belonging to the upper and the rising strata of the Turkish society, you will still see links with the past, an uninterrupted continuity in the living time capsule so indicative of the life in Istanbul. We had many callers, apart from friends, colleagues, neighbors, distant visitors, and acquaintances. They were the common Callers and some of them were Criers too. I want to tell you about them and show you their charms.

They were men, women, sometimes small groups. They passed by. They stopped. They called. They cried out offering their wares and their services. Sometimes they even came up. Some had horse carts, others mobile stalls. Still others had their wares on their backs (never on their heads) or strapped to their body. They came to sell or to buy. What they came to sell was made at home or produced at the farm or in the village or the woods, though sometimes these were also produced elsewhere. They came to buy what you no longer needed.

They came to sell to children and women mostly, but men too fell for them. What they sold was fresh, colorful, and attractive. It was also cheap. The Callers made the scene of life as lived in times gone by: you were the fresh arrival; they, the eternity of life.

There were different times for different Callers. Some came every day, some on weekdays only, others on Sundays. Still more came only on holidays or festival days. In the case of some, winter was their time. Others came only in summer. Some were seasonal in their visits, depending upon when the fruit was ripe or when the winter was about to begin or summer make way for the autumn. Very rarely was there any competition among them—one of each type and one at a time. There was an established sequence for such Callers and the hours were known to all concerned. They never let you down and your expectations were always fulfilled.

When you heard *simiticii* call out "*Simiti, simiti*" you had to rush out to look as others did, and buy and eat as you walked or stood. *Simit* is the crisp, brown ring of bread baked with seeds of sesame. This is carried on a stick, held high so that the rings will not fall. The further supplies are in a container with glass around it, strapped to his body. He also has strapped to himself in the front a pouch of coins in which he will drop what he receives from you and out of which he will fetch out the change that he must give when necessary. You bought quickly, you paid quickly, and quickly you began to eat because he was in a hurry to move on. As he moved you heard his call and the jingle of his coins. He had a circuit and the beat must be completed within a certain time limit, while the *simiti* was warm, while his customers were waiting for his call. *Simiti* is a part of the democratic scene of life in Turkey; even the rich buy it and eat it.

Another Caller was a real sight. He was the *baloncu*, flying gas-filled balloons of different colors and sizes. Walking and hawking. His cry was music to the ears of children, but the children were up in their flats. So the windows opened and heads popped out to call the balloon man to stop. The man below gave out his price. The choice was made. And then the balloon began to rise higher and higher (it was on a string, as you would have guessed) until it reached exactly where the window had opened. There the exchange was made. The mother took over the string and with it the balloon. Through the window the string passed into the hands of the child and the balloon continued its flight upward. The mother then threw down the coin, which was picked up by the balloon man. So went the purchase.

On the left of our block the street was a cobbled one, and when any horse cart went on it we could hear it. By and by we began also to recognize from afar what the horse cart would be carrying and who the Caller would be. We could also see what was laid on it even from a distance—one of the gains of being on the thirteenth floor!

In summer, the horse cart would be loaded with watermelons, and the cry would go out—*karpuzcuu*. The horse cart would come right up to the midpoint of the two blocks. Men and women would go down to choose, to bargain, to buy, to weigh, and to pay. Then they would go up with a supply of melons, good enough for a week, carried in their trail by either the *kapici* or the seller of melons. This would go on for an hour or two. Then the seller of melons would come up, eventually to our floor, offering a selection of melons. Once more, the bargain over price and then the customary determination of weight in a country scale and then the transfer of the purchase for the price paid. The seller of melons would come practically every week, between a certain starting date and a certain closing date. But he would bring only red melons.

The white melons were brought by another seller, never the two at the same time. His call was also a different one—*kavuncuu*. And then the same sale and purchase took place, week after week. Everyone waited for them because their melons were especially sweet.

At a certain time of the year, on the occasion of a joyous Turkish and Moslem festival, you would find flocks of sheep being led by way of the cobbled street, coming from the open beyond, stopping at midpoint and slowly moving out and away from the housing area. At these midpoints you would also notice one of the two persons (he was the *coban*—shepherd) leading a sheep (most probably a ram) or two or even three and disappearing in another block, returning with nothing on his leash, only money in his pocket. The sheep had been sold to the expectant purchasers at their doorsteps.

Then the flock would move on to another block. The word would go 'round by the "bebe bebe" of the sheep (the cry of the Callers) and the rich ones would come out and quietly, expertly, with the participation of the *kapici*, make their purchase. In a case or two the sheep would be taken inside the home if it were on the ground floor or at the basement. In other cases it would be tied at the rear, but there were occasions, special ones concerning the rich buyers, when the tying would be done just adjacent to the outer doorstep. Then for a day or two one heard, high up on the thirteenth floor, the "bebe bebe, bebe bebe" of the new house guests.

The same day or the next, but never later than that, someone would come not to sell but to offer his services. These would be the *kasap* (butchers) offering their professional expertise. Once more the price would be fixed and a contract made. Then on the appointed day, you would hear the joyous festival dawn commencing with the cries of the led ones and then the slaughtered ones. And when you came down you saw blood flowing (even some slaughter in progress), and lying around in pools, in and out of where you walked. Three or four days later, depending upon the weather conditions, the blood would dry up, leaving red marks of the festival. These would become brown and then black in days ahead. Then dust would lie over them and hide what lay buried beneath.

The *plastikci* would come with plastic wares on a hand wagon. He would neither cry out nor call. He would wait in the outer space for you to come. As the sun went up his colorful display would be attractive enough. The hand wagon was full of articles for household needs. And when these can be met at the doorstep, what more must be asked when the price too is reasonable? Plastic wash basins, jerry cans, buckets, watering hose, water jugs would all be sought out by the ladies of the area. On this occasion there was rarely a haggle over the price.

Likewise there would be another hand cart full of footwear—brought by the *ayakkabici*—plastic, leather, rubber, shoes, sandals, inner wear, outer wear, rainwear, cheap wear, for men, women, and children. In this case too there would be no call, but the sale would not be a quick one. There would be this one to try, that one to take home for the grandmother to try, three or four pairs would be taken inside. It was rarely a matter of size—try and fit was the practice. It was which color. Which price. Fashion was important.

The flower woman came almost every week and you loved to hear her "*Cicekci.*" She called out and then stayed on the ground to offer you a bouquet or a bunch or a flower, of this kind and that. But hardly any with perfume or fragrance. Color, youth, abundance. She stayed the whole morning or the whole afternoon, never the whole day. Sometimes she came up to tempt you with the call. She always came with bouquets in her hand, and no one refused her. When she came you bought. Sometimes as I passed by her sitting place, she would offer me a bouquet and a separate offer of a flower, a colorful one for my Golden Retriever, and she would tie it to his collar.

Callers of fruit came when fruit was abundant, cheap, ripe, and good. But each seller would have only one variety. At one time it would be cherries, another day strawberries. When peaches appeared and pears too, these would be brought in hand carts and sold in bulk. In season came apples and oranges. When Washingtons (the larger orange variety) came, purchases were made for the week.

The nicest fruit and the most famous one, the black figs, soft, sweet, and tender, were, however, not brought to your doorstep by any one Caller or Crier or anyone at all. Their tenderness and ripeness demanded that your desire for them should lead you to the special shops where they could be had at their best. There you went almost every day while the season lasted.

Like fruit, vegetables also came. Tomatoes sometimes came with cauliflower, the two together. There would be onions and artichokes and potatoes alone. The vegetables in Istanbul were emperor size; the eggplant, the *aubergine*, and the *patlican* of Istanbul were royal in appearance, rich in color.

Sometimes callers came with a small tractor and a pickup attached to it, selling several kinds of vegetables, all from the farm of the owner-driver. Sometimes it would be a man with a horse cart selling one or two or even three items together. At other times it would be a man with a hand cart selling only one particular vegetable. They would call out the name of the vegetable, then at a short interval the name of another vegetable would be heard, but when the seller had many kind of vegetables to offer, he would in quick succession call out one name after another.

The *sutcuu*, *yogurtcuu*, and *peynircii* came with their cans. They brought milk, yogurt, and cheese. Many waited for them and continued to prefer their creations to those sold in shops, bottled and pasteurized though these may be.

The bear man, *ayici*, came, calling out, announcing his arrival with a walk of gaiety. The children rushed out, the women opened their windows. He began to show the dance of the Russian bear at the Turkish doorstep and made the bear obey that which no man, Russian or another, would do to anyone's bidding. It was a sight! There he was to entertain and to instruct, more important than either to buy or to sell.

On a horse-driven cart came the man *saksici* to sell you earthen flower pots (baked and those not so well baked) and mother earth too if you so wished.

Then there was the cassette man. Although he did not come to our area, I met him and several of his class at other places, particu-

The Turkish barber talks as he cuts or shaves, with his cutthroat moving in and out in one hand, the other hand keeping company by making empty gestures. Sometimes with both hands waving in air, he talks to you, to his colleagues, to the new arrivals, even to himself. Should the mood persist, he even sings a tune.

While he talks you cannot talk, much less talk back. You must know what he has in hand and why he is talking all the time. He is a barber and a talker, both by profession. He decides what you should have and he does it to you. Argue if you like, but beware of your throat. While cutting and talking, he does a third thing, too. He watches you. And not only you, he watches everyone, even what is going on in the corridor.

As a man of religion, depending upon how young you are and how old he is, he might have even been the performer of your circumcision. Between himself and yourself, it is a man-to-man affair.

If he wanted he could perhaps be silent even when your head or face or both are covered in copious Turkish towels, but if he did so he would let down the tradition of the sultan's barber. How can he be so rude? Lest you may have missed something in news or gossip or opinion he will bring you up to date. He will tell you where to go and for what and will answer all your secret desires with a smile. The Turkish barber is the man for you.

10. Recreation

IN ISTANBUL everyone swims all the time, rich and poor, time or no time, transport or no transport, planning or no planning. There is sunshine for eight months of the year, and swimming for six months. Swimming is a way of life. It does not even matter which side of the Bosphorus you are on or whether you live in town or out. The *dolmus* (public transport by car), the bus, and the ferry will take you where you want to go. You can walk too, depending on how close you are. Apart from the Bosphorus and its terminal ends, there are the Black Sea and the Sea of Marmara. Swimming was, is, and will always be a way of life in Istanbul, and the physical beauty of the Turk seems at its best when he is swimming.

Like many cities in Europe and elsewhere, Istanbul has woods where people go to picnic, breathe fresh air, play, show off their love of nature, and generally do something different from swimming, sunning, eating, talking, and just living. But these woods, the Belgarde Forest, are not close by and so the distance is covered either in one's own car or in the *dolmus*. But unlike woods elsewhere, these woods are for family pleasure only.

The woods of Istanbul are not for lovers, present or future. There are no trees where you can hide or seek and none to give you cover when you need it most if you are a lover and you have someone to bestow your love upon. You cannot even go there at night. No one does. The trees stand as custodians of Turkish moral standards. The open spaces in the woods are exclusively for use as family picknicking grounds.

There are other custodians too. These are the forest guards and the security guards, who watch. It does not matter who you are or where you are, the watch is everlasting. How effective it was, especially during the times of the martial law!

The basketball court was in front of my apartment, a common court where teams could play and beginners learn. We enjoyed many moments of fun watching the Turks play basketball, jumping up and down, slipping in and out. Teams from different parts of the city used to come to play matches. So we saw the city too, right under our noses.

Football was also close by. Almost next to my office was the sports stadium, and well before the day of the match, I planned carefully when to go to the office, how early to leave, and how early to return. Quite some strategy also went into the planning of the route to take. The match day was a special day for all. When a goal was scored or missed, two things happened almost simultaneously. One was the shouting that went up and the other was the special cry and clap of the Turk. Depending upon the style of the shout and the tone of the clap and its frequency and duration, one came to know whether it was the Turks who had scored or whether it was the Turks who had failed to win. (This was when the match was between the Turks and the teams from abroad.) National pride was respected in every possible way. When there was a football match involving outsiders and the Turks (sometimes even when Turks were not involved and even when the match was not at Istanbul), practically no male student was available for study, for food, for parental response, not even for lovemaking. They were watching the TV.

Why they played no other games was not difficult to guess: the Turk wants something or someone to kick or to push. The ball was the best. The ball if you play tennis or the ball when you play cricket was not the ball that the Turk wanted. Not even the golf ball. These games were not manly enough. The Turk had no fancy for fancy games, and some thought that even basketball would be dropped soon enough with the fall of the last ball in the net. There was less and less space for basketball courts and practically every one of these was being pushed to the outskirts or inner yards. The football grounds too were getting fewer and fewer. What will the Turks then do? Play other games? Or go elsewhere to play them? Even the *International Herald Tribune* felt the compulsion to print a picture of a large-sized basketball court and write "Thanks to Theodosius—Lacking playgrounds in the old city of Istanbul, these youngsters [shown in the picture] have set up their field just outside the crumbling city walls, which were built by Theodosius II in 413, when the city was Constantinople."

Should you go there now, however, you will find that even this field has moved. To keep the play moving, the fields keep moving too, though not for the same reason. The ground on which the fields are set up is of greater value to the Turks than the value they attach to the play of their children. This is exactly what happened to the basketball court in front of our apartment. The land was sold, new blocks came up, and the proceeds were divided among those who had claim to the land. Not a word of protest or a voice of anger at what was disappearing to make way for what had appeared. But you must not judge harshly. It may not have been the love of money (who does not love what one needs) alone. You must also know of the love of the Turk for the sacred land with its fragrance and content of history. How could such land be put to less valuable a use!

Now from the particular to the general. The rich, the sophisticated, and the educated have many ways to occupy their leisure time. Istanbul's Asian side is generally for the poor, but insofar as the rich are concerned, some of the leading pleasure areas are on the Asian side. The Bosphorus makes certain that the Asian side of Istanbul is truly apart from the European side, though with the ferry boats and now the Bridge of Bosphorus, the in and out has become more frequent. The rich like it so. The Asian side of the Black Sea, across the Bosphorus, knows how to satisfy the desires of the rich. The Sea of Marmara also knows not only its ways but also the ways of the rich.

And then there are the islands. The least important one has, according to storytellers, been used to starve out stray (and not so stray) dogs by the thousand, at one time. Another one, more important, is for the training of the Navy. The third one for some third use. But the biggest and the best of them all, the Buyuk Ada, is for the richer, the more sophisticated, the educated, and also in particular for the leaders of minorities such as the Jews, the Druses, the Greeks, and the Armenians who have their villas and clubs there.

The Turks and their army also have their share of the resources of the Buyuk Ada. On the Asian side of the seas and the waterfronts and on the Buyuk Ada, the rich go for their vacations and longer stays, having had the best of winter, autumn, and spring in their Istanbul homes. They go there, bag and baggage, to their summer houses—this includes their boys and girls, who are free from schools for most of summer and free from many other things too. So the boys and girls meet on the pleasure grounds, for weeks on end (not only on weekends as otherwise might be the case), swimming, playing, strolling, chatting, gazing, basking, relaxing, eating, yielding, with sun above them, and enjoying the proximity which the light of the moon makes possible on summer nights. This is the time when the fathers are away to make more and more at Istanbul, the mothers cannot watch from the balconies (in any case the mothers are too busy in their own mature ways), the grandmothers and the grandfathers have been left behind to have some freedom at last, and all brothers and sisters are doing exactly what every boy and girl is doing. So it is freedom for all.

II. Driving

YOU SHOULD KNOW about the driving in Istanbul in some detail. Driving in Istanbul drives you crazy, because the other drivers in your mature judgment are crazy. The craziness is overpowering and so widespread that even the Turks from Ankara are afraid of driving in Istanbul.

Why is it crazy? First, the background. No old car is ever abandoned in Istanbul; this would offend the Turkish tradition. That is why you will see all shapes and forms and makes and years of cars in Istanbul. You will find vintage cars on the roads of Istanbul, not in special rallies. The Turks have a special genius for making their cars behave themselves. Just as an apartment can take so many persons, so can some of the roads, streets, and lanes of Istanbul. But the maximum limit was exceeded a long, long time ago. And there is no way of avoiding one road to take another, or one street for another, and even one lane for the next. A lot of them are all that you have.

Turkish-made Renaults and Fiats, besides the Mercedes, the Volkswagens, the Chevrolets, the Buicks, the Oldsmobiles, by the hundreds (some say 2,000, some say more) are added to the traffic of Istanbul every month. You need a calculating mind to total up all that this means in a city with its ancient and crowded complexion. Next to having your own apartment (and a summer house), having a car is a status symbol, just as much as having a respectable wife confers respectability.

Every driver—this will include you, too—is in a hurry. It does not matter whether the car can do it or not, whether the road is going up or down, whether there is no room to move ahead at all, whether right is wrong or wrong is right. The driver is in a hurry and this is what you must know. The more you know the more crazy you become. Every driver becomes crazy soon after he takes over the wheel, and when one crazy meets another and more meet more, the more crazy you find each of them. To overtake, you need not look left, right, behind, or in front. Just overtake, even if an inch is all you gain. If you rub someone's shoulder, it is never your fault. Why should the shoulder have been jutting out and even why was the shoulder so large? So you fear no one.

A car in front of you will slow down without reason or indication. It will even come to sudden halt. That is because someone wanted to get out. And for this it would not be necessary for the car to pull in. No, as you were. He stops and you stop and everyone stops. Then when he moves, you move. Equally, if you find someone who looks like he might need a ride, beware because someone will pick him up, again without pulling in. Sometimes, while the car is still moving, in and out will take place. It is the Turkish *dolmus* and you must respect its democratic right to do this and more. A fire engine may make way for you, but not a Turkish *dolmus*. It would be against the ethics of the road. There are no horns, but be prepared for shouts. These do have an effect, you know. The minibuses will also show you their strength. They run on an extremely tight schedule, coming and going in and out of Istanbul. The trucks must also roll by. The trade depends on them. Horse carts have a right of way. Cars are parked in your way, or break down. This calls for greater vigilance.

You must make way for a Mercedes, as the car with the highest priority next to *dolmus*—unless of course there is a car with the Turkish flag or with a police siren. Next to Mercedes come all other big cars, mostly American. So if you want a priority without being an American, the next best way to have it is to have an American car. Then comes the horse-driven cart carrying melons, vegetables, fruit, etc. At the tail end are the Fiats and the Renaults.

If you hit someone, shout the most and the loudest and frighten others by your demeanor and authority, gestures, words, and pitch of anger. If you are yourself hit, do the same and more, so that at least one of the crowd will agree to be your witness. One day I saw such hit-and-miss between two public buses. Even the passengers of the buses joined in the fray, taking sides not on the side of right or against the one who was in the wrong but whether one was in this or that bus. Finally both public buses went their public way.

You should be prepared for brow-beating, scaring, pushing, puffing, growling, shoving, roughing, crowding, shouting, and snarling when you are in someone's way. Never be in the way of a Turk when he is driving or when he is making love. He is then at his best. You must also never forget that you are in his country, something which he does not wish to be reminded about. You are dealing not only with driving. You are dealing with character, psychology, freedoms, and above all, with tradition. When you know a little more, even if it be not all, you will also realize that this is not the occasion to be a cry baby. If that is all you are, don't ever step in.

12. *Dolmus*

You can have a ride in a car without owning it or driving it. It need not belong to any of your parents or relatives, friends, colleagues, or neighbors. It is hitchhiking of a more orderly, organized, and established kind. The car belongs to someone and is driven by someone else, but it is not a taxi. It is much more (or much less in many ways). You cannot occupy the whole of it, though you and your friends and even your family can take the whole of it, provided you take seat by seat and each of you occupies no more than one seat. But you must go its way. It will not turn or twist at your command, no matter how much you may try or pay. It is very cheap. It is like the current of water or the current of air. If you go along with it, you can float or fly. But if you cross its path, then you are on your own. It is the Turkish *dolmus*, but you must not confuse it with similar facilities in Beirut or Jerusalem or elsewhere. You will soon see why.

The *dolmus* has fixed routes and pathways. Within limits it goes from point to point, however long or short the points may be from each other. It starts and ends at predetermined and well-known crossroads of traffic. It generally commences and ends its journey on schedule. It does not pull out or pull in to drop you by the curb. This is your own concern. It will take you where there are two lanes. But if it is one way, he knows the way. When there is no lane ahead, he will take you that far but no more.

The *dolmus* way is known only to Turkey. The *dolmus* can pass through the eye of a needle, through the eye of a hurricane too. It knows all the arteries and the veins of Istanbul. It is as old as the oldest automobile in this part of the world, highly respected and respectfully treated, even by the Turkish system. All main routes of Istanbul are covered by the *dolmus*. If you have the *dolmus* map, you do not need the street map at all. Just follow the *dolmus* and it will take you to all worthwhile places. The *dolmus* has followed its route and its way unchanged, and the story goes that new buildings and new roads have had to respect the ways of the *dolmus* while determining their own. If you wish to hop, you can do so from one *dolmus* to another. You can thus go from end to end in Istanbul; you can go where you want. You can take a *dolmus* to Europe and do it faster than most. Every night a new crew will take you through while you rest and relax. You say where you want to stop, and he will stop for you. Every place is a flag station.

The *dolmus* ride is a fixed-price ride from point to point or all the way through. No negotiations, no meter, no tip, no quarrel. You pay in silence and you ride in silence. It is like a private, almost a personal car with no ticket given or kept. You are relieved of all transport problems and all traffic responsibilities— no third-party risk insurance, no parking meters or fees. When you travel by *dolmus*, you pay at the end of the journey (sometimes at the beginning, if you are in a hurry, or even in between the start and the end), just as you would when in a taxi. The cash is placed on top of a Turkish towel for all to see as it rests between the windscreen and the dashboard. When the cash bag reveals its open face, the *dolmus* is on a long trip. You and your fellow passengers collect what each must pay, and, when it seems enough, the chosen one hands it over to the leader, who hands it all to the driver.

The poor use it always. The distances are long. Istanbul is all up or down or both, walking takes time and is not the most elegant mode of travel. Those who are not so poor also use the *dolmus* because it is so convenient and so cheap. The rich also avail themselves of the opportunity to go by it. It is safe. It waits for no one. You must wait for it and if it has room, it will come near you but if there is no seat it will go by without a smile. Should you accost it, politely or rudely, and there is no room, you will be informed by the classic "unspoken no." However, if your luck is with you, the door will open to let you in. It is the most democratic form of conveyance by car. The rich may have their own but they pay for it too. City folk and village women are all alike. The *dolmus* greets no one on arrival or on descent. You cannot hire it. You can only ride in it.

The *dolmus* has no sympathy for you when you are about to be married or just married, and do not expect it to make its way for you either. But once you have children—whether you are married, or when you were married, if at all (the driver does not concern himself with your private life)—he will pick them up from your place, take them to school, and bring them back to your home, all in good company, on time, safe, and without breach of promise. You can trust him as the custodian of your children. Several *dolmus* drivers take upon themselves these sacred duties, every morning and every afternoon as long as the schools are open and as long as there are children who wish to attend them. And the cost is no more than what it always has been or will be—the lowest possible. This is one occasion on which the *dolmus* bends its way to find the shortest way to the nearest school.

13. Orient Express

ISTANBUL MADE THE ORIENT EXPRESS FAMOUS, though the Orient Express also added to the fame of Istanbul. Stories, songs, and jokes about Constantinople and colorful spy stories linking the Orient Express and Istanbul have added to the fame of both Istanbul and the Orient Express. It was called the Orient Express because it ran between Europe and the Orient. If your intentions were honorable, you enjoyed the journey. If they were not, you profited from it. As neutrality has conferred untold boons upon those who know how to practice the art, the Orient Express conferred its favors upon Istanbul, most certainly, but upon others too. It took you to the Orient and even when you stopped at the gateway, at Istanbul, you were already in the midst of the Orient, with its past, present, and future.

Who came by the Orient Express (and who went)? Hippies, persons not so rich, the young wanting to rough it out, families with baggage, those who wanted to test the fame of the Orient Express and the fame of its route, those who wished to stop en route or join others en route, others who had undisclosed interests and destination, of course also those who wanted to travel in the old style of luxury. Some waited days seeking tickets and reservations at Istanbul, lying on the platform as bodies ready to be transported. Others came at the moment of departure, to slip in. Some talked and talked with unknown companions en route, others remained exclusive even among themselves. Sometimes even the nobility, for presumably noble reasons, took the Orient Express. The number of those who came from the east of Turkey to take the Orient Express was not large. Equally, those who came from the West to go onward beyond Turkey was also not large —a changing pattern.

Istanbul was the terminus of an international rail service on its European side. On the Asian side, Istanbul was and continues to be the start of the Baghdad Railway. Baghdad Railway took over from where the Orient Express left. What a continuity!

The Orient Express served Istanbul and the Turks in many ways. They could bring all they wanted under their personal custody along with themselves and their families, from anywhere in Europe and beyond when they came to Istanbul. No other way of transport could do for them what the Orient Express did. The Turk does not like to part with his belongings. If he sent them by truck, he and his belongings would be separated. If he was driving his car, there were limits to what the car could carry. If he sent it by air, apart from the cost, here too he would have to part company with his belongings. Even if he came by boat, since Istanbul happened to open up this possibility too, his heavy baggage would have to be consigned to the hold. So the Orient Express, being an express as well, was "after his heart."

Knowing these happy ways of the Turk, The *International Herald Tribune* wrote on its most enjoyed last page, even after the Orient Express discontinued its total run of the good old days:

> If you wondered why the Donan Express (Cologne–Istanbul) ran late over the week end, it was because a homeward bound Turk wanted to take one-and-a-half tons of baggage along. As he stuffed the goods in his compartment, infuriated passengers, clambering over the stacked trunks and suitcases, protested to the conductor. The Turk and his tonnage were hauled off the train at Remorgem, 30 miles down the line, by eight Railway cops, and eventually he was persuaded to load the bulk on to a freight car (the man had a complete automobile and household with him).

The nostalgia of the Orient Express not only continues but is growing, and fresh ideas to bring back the Orient Express and the route to Istanbul emerge from time to time. Here is one of the latest ones, in the style of the past—the murder, the acting, and the spice of romance, mystery and life. The idea is to charter a train from French Railways for a ten-day return trip from Paris to Istanbul during which the guests dress up in 1920s clothes and solve a murder to be staged by twelve actors. The person who solves the murder will get back the cost of his fare!

14. Centers

THERE ARE UNLIMITED WAYS OF KNOWING Istanbul, and the more ways you follow the more you will find and understand. If you would go back a century or two and find the silk lace made by the convent nuns of those times, you could, holding the lace in the palm of your hand, follow the lines and the intricate design of it to see what Istanbul has to show to someone like you. It is in these lacy lanes that the network of life, interlinked and yet independent, goes on as it has always done.

Each family, and within it each member, is a universe, self-contained and upright, held together in its independent way, into a tribe. The tribe makes the village on the plains of Anatolia and the tribe makes the lanes inside the bowels of earth of Istanbul. Independent, apart, and interconnected. When you come out of the lanes onto the streets and then to the roads and the highways, you will see what holds the past and the present together. As each tribe is the source of strength, so is each lane a castle with its moat and a fort, with its points for battle and points for escape and retreat. With such identity, traditions, and the weight of the past, to arrive at the present has itself taken a long time. With its own center of gravity, Istanbul is also the center of gravity of Turkey, though the balance of power is held by Ankara; but Ankara is only the fulcrum. Although Istanbul has Byzantine intrigue and Oriental ways, it is also as modern as the shine on your face.

Istanbul has many centers of importance, and each such center must be identified, demarcated, visited, and its characteristics understood, as this will contribute to your understanding of the Turkish way of life. For instance, within a few kilometers of each other (you can walk the distance in twenty minutes) you can move from Taksim to Elmadag on to Harbiye, to Pangalti, to Osman Bey, reach Sisli and Mecidiyekoy, and a few more minutes of effort will take you to Gayerettepe, Essentepe, and Zingirli-kuyu. In these few minutes you would have walked through quarters of great significance.

Taksim

Everyone in Istanbul knows Taksim. Outside too in Turkey, many know it and even those who do not have either heard of it or read about it. So when we arrived in the city of Istanbul, we asked for the way to Taksim, as our hotel was near there. We asked at each important road site and finally we got there. After a stay of a few days in Istanbul, we realized why we had not been able to get to Taksim so easily. It was not the fault of those who directed us. It was not the fault of any, ourselves included. You could reach Taksim in many ways, taking different directions, even opposite directions. We were looking for the Taksim Square. Square it may be, but it is more a circle; Rather, it is a point—a point of history, a point of destiny, pinnacle of glory, crest of history. Taksim is also the way of life. The past, the present, and the future converge at Taksim. That is why they just say Taksim and you should know what they mean by it.

Almost eight different directions lead to Taksim, and if you are devious enough there are many more ways of getting in and out. The two most important shopping streets and several important localities and quarters of Istanbul make a beginning from this all-important and significant Taksim. There is a *dolmus* from Taksim for wherever you want to go. A bus will take you to Taksim from any direction. The airlines are in the vicinity. The hotels are either on the spot or within easy reach. You climb up to Taksim. If you wish, you can go down too. The German consulate is 'round the corner, so is the French consulate. The British consulate and the American consulate and several other missions are not far away. The Opera House is there (built, burned down, and built again, all in no time). You can also find a Turkish Bath. The travel agents and the tourist buses will pick you up and leave you at Taksim. Whatever you seek, you will find there.

Every political meeting of importance starts at Taksim and ends at Taksim. Taksim has seen the fall of prime ministers and the rise of new ones with the meetings addressed there. From Taksim you can behold the past, too. Everyone goes to Taksim.

So you will meet the East and the West and the Middle East. Those who were governed from Taksim in the past and those who form the basis of government today will all be found at Taksim. Taksim is a continuing link with history. In the Turkish language Taksim means division—to divide into parts.

Istiklal Caddesi

Having known Istanbul's Taksim and the Taksim of Turkey, it is essential also to know Istiklal Caddesi (the freedom street, street of independence, or street of liberty), which flows out of Taksim to its destined end. When you go down it, you come to Beyoglu and then you proceed farther down and you come to a tunnel and then out of the tunnel (a short underground run in a three-carriage train). You are almost at the Galata Bridge, which has the Golden Horn on its right. You could do it the other way too and climb up from the bottom to the top.

When we arrived the traffic went both ways: *dolmus*, taxis, cars, horse carriages. But the street of freedom did not have room enough for two traffic lanes, and so, two or three years after our stay, it became one-way traffic from the bottom to the top, to Taksim. Istiklal Caddesi is a street of historical fame, a landmark, and of continuing importance.

It is essentially a flowing stream of human beings. In one walk, going down or going up, the type and variety of people you meet are unique. A time comes when you do not walk: you follow; you proceed, slow step by slow step. You must watch what is ahead of you, and while you may brush each other, you must not push. You must also avoid being moved faster than you can afford to move forward. You will see people from different parts of Turkey. You will meet Armenians, Greeks, Cypriots, Bulgarians, Russians, Americans, English, Germans, French, Israelis, Jews, Druses, Europeans of different nationalities. You will meet people who are there for the day, for a moment. People from cities, towns, villages. People doing business, or gazing or strolling. People going to eat. People going to do their shopping. People looking at each other. Different costumes, different dresses, even different civilizations. Men, women, young, old, boys, girls.

The best cinemas are there, the excellent shoe shops, the department stores, the standing places, the climbing alleys. You will find a Turkish bath. You will find vendors on the footpaths. You will find seekers and searchers. Pharmacies, opticians, dressmakers, barbers, sellers of toys and clothes and all there is to offer. At the end of Istiklal Caddesi you will find the Balak Bazaar, which means the fish market, but here you will also find the sellers of fruit, vegetables, flowers, and the meats and cheeses and yogurts of Turkey.

Should you look around, you will then find the British Consulate in all its permanent glory, with its enclosed quarters for the staff and the Rolls-Royce that goes in and out. If you go downward a little more, there will be the consulates of Sweden, the Netherlands, and many more.

All this may be charming, but I went through the wide variety of streets and lakes that lead you out of Istiklal Caddesi. At the bottom of the pit are the homes of the hundreds and thousands of those who have not yet surfaced fully, who live in the old dilapidated homes, in unexpected overcrowding. Once in these zones you see the hidden poor, the womb of Istanbul which has not yet delivered.

You could never persuade anyone to tell you, exactly where what you were seeking would be on the Istiklal Caddesi. I tried at the office, in the neighborhood, and among my friends, even after I knew them well. The reply always was to go to Istiklal Caddesi. If I persisted and asked, is it close to this, or is it at the beginning, end, or in between, on the right from where you go down or on the left as you come up, the reply always was the same. It is at Istiklal Caddesi.

Sisli

This is another terminus of the shopping streets that go from Taksim to Sisli (on almost the opposite side of Istiklal Caddesi). What lies at the back of the shopping streets, on either side, is also generally called Sisli.

There are two unique things that stand out about the journey from Taksim to Sisli. The first one (this ended after a year or two) was how to walk across the street. Not only were there no traffic lights and no policemen on duty, but the moving vehicles will wait for no one. I tried the usual method of raising the hand. No one stopped. Then I observed how others did it. They waited until more people joined them and when they had become a crowd, two or three or four deep, they made a concerted effort, almost holding hands, daring the traffic from one end to the other end of the street. They ran, hopeful that human mass would not be trampled. Quickly the move was made and the journey accomplished.

The second unique matter of Sisli was that when you proceeded by car from Taksim in the direction of Sisli, before you realized it, you were already on a street that was called something else. This street was followed by another, again called by another name. Then followed still another name, again followed by one more name. This was not to be the end. Some more names and some more streets, and soon you found yourself at Sisli. This was all in straight line, one following the other in rapid sequence, and the whole journey completed in a few minutes when the traffic was in your favor.

Galatasary Passage

While in Istanbul you will often cross the Galata Bridge. You will also see the Galata Tower from time to time. You may make friends, and some are bound to be from the Galatasary School.

When this happens you will find yourself in the midst of a special group that comes from the Galatasary School, people old enough now to be in charge of many affairs of Istanbul, some even of Turkey.

There is still some more of Galata—the Galatasary Passage, a passage, an enclosure, an enclave, an institution, a must for everyone who wishes to know Istanbul. There are the journalists, the groups who meet to drink and discuss, the individuals who do not wish to go straight home from work, all and sundry who wish a quick drink of beer, some mussels to go with it, on occasion shrimp and lobster. In an atmosphere of ancient times and tradition, in light which shines one way all the time, with tables and benches on which have sat your predecessors and ancestors, in a place where talk flows freely and friendships are formed quickly.

Take a Bavarian beer hall, add to it what could possibly be added of the British pub. Follow through with the old Middle East *saray*, and let these three meet in the midst of Istanbul. This is the Galatasary Passage.

Mecidiyekoy–Gayerettepe–Essentepe– Zingirli-kuyu

These are four quarters of an ancient city, all within walking and shouting distance of each other. In addition to their earlier importance, they have been given more importance because all the Bosphorus Bridge traffic and much more touches them and passes through them. The new roadways have brought these areas out of their earlier deep slumber or unawareness and thrown them into the future. Trucks follow each other, day and night.

I lived in Gayerettepe and saw it come of age. You too should go to see what more has happened in order to understand this new dimension superimposed on these quarters, even on Istanbul as a whole.

15. Boy Meets Girl

THEY FIND EACH OTHER in the apartment block in which they live or in the street or the lane in which they reside. Many do. It could be at the university, and a particularly successful one may be at the Bosphorus College (Roberts College, as it is still called by the Americans and the old-timers). Many go to the Bosphorus cafés, especially in summer. Crowds gather and you may meet your mate. Friends of friends are another possibility; relatives also help in these times. But the special flavor of Istanbul comes out best when I tell you what I was told—a person-to-person account of what did in fact happen and how it happened.

She told me herself after we had been friends for some years. She was living on the Asian side of the Bosphorus and on every working day used to take an early-morning ferry to come over to the European side, take a *dolmus*, and then climb up the steep steps to the office and be in time at the opening hour of eight o'clock Monday to Friday, each week. It was always the same ferry, leaving at the same time. It all went as scheduled unless there was some special situation that called for a change.

She suddenly, one morning, noticed a person on the ferry. She saw the same person on the following morning, too. This went on for a week or so. Then she took greater note of this person: how he looked, what he was wearing. She watched him from time to time, at intervals, each morning. This went on for some time and then their eyes met.

Then they moved nearer each other. Days later, they sat together. Then they exchanged "*Merhaba*" (Hello), "*Gunaydin*" (Good Morning). As days went by one word followed another. It became conversation, dialogue, question and answer. One thing led to another. The *dolmus* journey, after leaving the ferry, was then done together. Coffee on the boat. Coffee at the café, later.

One day to another. *Nishan* (engagement) followed. And then came *nikah* (wedding). All in a few weeks of that warm summer. All because the ferry started at the same time every day!

Another account was given to me by my wife, who had heard it from her dear friend, as it is easier for ladies to speak of their hopes and expectations among themselves. She took a five-day trip as a holiday in summer on a boat (this is how she had met her first husband, too). She met him there; he was from the navy. Since he loved the sea, he had taken the trip to enjoy a holiday on the sea free from discipline and work. He entered into another discipline, though. They were engaged and married soon after their return from the trip. For him, too, it was the second time. They were our neighbors across the street.

Another one was in the last year of school; we had seen her grow up, being close neighbors in the same apartment block. We saw the change overtaking her; she revealed herself more and more in the less and less that she wore as the summer came along. Soon she disappeared. She went on a five-day holiday boat trip and when she returned, she had what she wanted. Soon there was *nishan* and then marriage, while the school continued. After some weeks she passed her second examination. Both took a small flat opposite our block and we saw them come and go all the time, this bride with her groom visiting her parents. Seekers will find, and the Turks have reason to be proud not only of their seas but also of the five-day holiday boat trips on these seas!

16. What Are You Looking For?

Sooner or later, the conversation came round to marriage with almost every student (first the boys and then the girls). Yes, I want to marry, but there is no hurry. It did not seem to be a matter of concern until about thirty-five years of age. Also, in one shape or another the question then put was, "What are you looking for?" or "Whom would you like to marry?" Almost a total consensus seemed to exist among boys of different size, shape, form, and different educational and family backgrounds, ages, and occupations. The consensus may be summarized in the following way, which is indicative of priorities, presenting a complete picture of the sought-after wife-to-be.

1. She must be able to look after the home very well.
2. She must be a good cook.
3. She must be able to bring up my children very well.
4. She must come from a wealthy family and her share of wealth must be considerable and well established. This is so that should (or when) the marriage break up, the judge will take her independent material situation into account and because of her own means of living, the alimony that may become due will be very little. The wife would not become a burden when she is wife no longer.
5. She should be able to keep a job when necessary, so that until there are children, there are two incomes to make a good home. Then, should (and when) the marriage break up, she could return to make her own living and the maintenance payable to her would be small.

But should she not be a virgin, as is made out to be an absolute prerequisite for every bride? This is taken for granted, and if she is not, the marriage will not follow through, even for a day. So it need not be mentioned. What of her age? She may be about ten years younger. What of physical beauty? Every Turkish girl is beautiful. But she must be healthy. Is not education important? Yes, but that is so that she can look after the children and keep a job. Anything else? Time will show.

When your bride-to-be must be a virgin and this is a prerequisite for marriage if it is to last even for one day, what of you? Being a virgin is not expected of men. Nor can it be a reason for not getting the best girl. On the contrary, my parents know it, her parents know it, she and her friends know it, her brother knows it—the more experienced the groom is, the more successful he will be when married.

When girl students were asked (many were asked, though the number was smaller than in the case of boys) the consensus seemed like this:

1. I want a husband.
2. He must be a man, mature and well placed.
3. He should be rich.

Other attributes and virtues? Handsome? All men are handsome. Job, wealth, car, apartment? Would he marry me if he did not have the items necessary for day-to-day living (if he does not have wealth or apartment, these will come; no matter for concern)? What of love? He knows it.

17. Marriage

IN ISTANBUL, and I guess in Ankara too, it was quite a thing to do —at least among the rich, the sophisticated, and the educated. It was to begin with *nishan* (engagement) and end with *nikah* (marriage ceremony according to the Moslem custom and religion), and finally, to complete the transaction, with civil marriage—that is, two ceremonies on the same day, of the same event, the same marriage. Civil marriage is compulsory in Turkey. That is the law.

Every day, many times a day, you can see private cars and taxis, large and small, flower decorated, going their way to the

Hall of Marriage, which is a facility widely used. It is a public hall where you meet your bride to join hands in wedlock in the presence of your friends, relatives, and parents under the official guide who finalizes what you set out to do. You sign and get out, without fuss, without much cost, without much ceremony. Quietly done is well done. Marriage is after all a commonplace event.

We came to know of some separations and divorces, but these had happened before we became neighbors. But on hearsay it can be mentioned that if getting married has become easy, getting divorced has also became easy. But the most admirable part of it all was the important fact that everyone was at peace with one another. The once permanent, sacred, important event had made way for the new realities of life.

There were several divorced persons in the blocks that made up my observation tower. These were mostly women, living alone. There were hardly any divorced men in these blocks. It was rather difficult to see the distinction between various types of divorce situations and those who were separated but not divorced. The divorced women did not find their chances for the next marriage to be dim. On the other hand, these did not seem to be bright either. That is why they were alone. But when they wanted to look around actively, they always moved out.

I could not ask the married men and women whom I knew well how their own yardsticks and benchmarks had worked out and what had been the highwater marks and the low in their own lives. It was for anyone to see, they would have said. I had, however, the opportunity to ask some of my men friends who had separated or divorced or were contemplating doing so to tell me a little about themselves. They did, adding that what was true of them was practically (I hope within limits) true of most. Here is what they said:

1. The turnover is the greatest before the firstborn; seldom after the second born.

2. In most cases it is even well before the firstborn.

3. It takes place almost always because there is a third one, either for him or for her (this did not result, however, in many cases insofar as women were concerned in early second marriage) but when it was the case of a fourth, one extra possibility for each one, remarriage took place in both cases.

4. Before the firstborn, the seductiveness still persists and so the chances of a new romance are brighter.

5. If the separation takes place early enough, the severance allowances are very small for the man to pay.

6. When there is no child, the maintenance pay is only for the woman and the period for which this may have to be paid may not be a long one.

7. The chances for second marriage (the third one was rather exceptional) again became the brightest at least for the woman when she was past the age of bearing any more children.

8. The husband who wanted to separate and get a divorce was very anxious that his overthrown wife should get married as quickly as possible to anyone at all and would even go out of his way to assist this process through friends and relatives.

Marriage with a woman who is marrying for the second time is a prize marriage, especially if she also has a child from another's efforts (some, however, prefer her without any child at all). This way, at the least cost, trouble, and future inconvenience should the marriage break up, the one marrying her (since he had already done his best before) was getting a woman, wife, and mother all in one, receiving all that a woman could give. To mention one more gain, a distinct one in the eyes of the beholder and the marrying one, the second-time wife would always do her best and be at her best to give her all. As regards the man, if he does not have the liability of a wife or a child, he is preferred by all. The once-married woman was always looking for a once-married man, but in the case of the man the entire field, even the university and the school campus, was open. Men had no embargo placed on them nor any time or age zone laid down for them.

A marriage, its disappearance, its replacement each took place in a very cool Turkish way. The Turk, man and woman, walked in and out, unruffled. It was, all along, a marriage without tears. If there was any calculation about it, it was more to avoid the costs of carryover.

18. Parents

PARENTS IN TURKEY are not just father and mother or just grand-father and grandmother. They are much more. Whether they are loved as much as they are obeyed and feared, they and their children alone know. But parents play a very important role from birth to death. And who one's parents are or were determines in a big way who would be what. If the father was a general (even a retired general) when the son grew up and was ready to be a man, the obedient son could certainly expect to go far, especially in the army should he wish to follow in papa's foot-steps. Or again, if the father was a man of riches or politics or religion, the son could certainly expect to be recognized equally as a man of riches or politics or religion. This was the hereditary way, the Turkish tradition.

There was, however, a but—the obedience part of it. Obedi-ence was the link, a living one between father and son, even more so than the fact of birth. The son learned everything from the father. The father was the giver of life and more. There was this obedience, therefore. Age did not matter. It was a lifelong link, and the life span in Turkey is generally very long indeed. There was obedience shown also to the mother, and love. This was visible and clear. The mother was also a parent, though respected for different reasons of different value. Then there was the sister. If she was older, she also received respect and love, if not obedience. A married sister was still a sister, though a brother's wife was another matter. Brother too was another matter.

The older the father and the mother became, the greater was the manifestation of respect. The home continued to be the home when both were together or when separation was forced upon one by the other or by the will of God. At the same time it was expected that the son would live apart to bring forward his sons (failing which, or in addition, daughters too). He would, however, irrespective of where he lived and what he did, be the son of his father and mother and be responsible to them and for them. When old age came, the merger took place and the grandpa, the grandma, the father, the mother, and the son and his wife and their children all lived together or in separate homes adjacent to each other. All made a great Turkish family, a strong, well-knit, and interdependent Turkish tribe.

That was the Turkish tradition, untouched and unmolested by the modern thoughts of the urban Turk, just as it continued to be the way of life in rural Turkey. When the daughter was married, the mother followed her to continue to look after her in her new home; sometimes the father too made it a point of daily visit (the same happened to them when their son got married and the mother-in-law followed).

When it came to looking after the father and the mother, whether they had wealth or not, irrespective of their needs of old age, it was invariably the son who showed love and assumed responsibility. It was the son who brought them over or went over to them and they lived together. In the case of the daughter, when the mother and the father were too old to be of any practical help or when their wealth was not enough to cover the cost of the responsibility, the daughter had her own family which came first, quite naturally you would say, would you not? But driven to it, the daughter would rather look after the mother than the father, whereas the son would look after both. Equality of opportunity must not be confused with equality of responsibility.

Parents were not regarded as a burden or a group to be avoided or to be separated from or to be visited only when in need. Parents were part of life, the same life even after marriage and when separate homes were made due to necessity. The parents continued to be as they were all along.

19. Retired Persons

RETIREMENT IN TURKEY does not mean that you have done something of which you should be ashamed, something which is not done, a matter of punishment and even regret. You do not hide it. You profit from it, if you will. Everyone retires, some even thrive on it. The age of retirement varies. In the armed services it is early enough to start another career. Retirement carries a good pension. A good part of one's salary becomes the pension for life. With retirement benefits you could build an apartment. You could grow an orchard. You could sail and swim. You will never sink though, because after a life of floating, there is no fear. Your children will look after you. As the head of the house you will be obeyed. You will never be in want, far from it. You will have all the time to be at home, to gossip, to waste time, to laze and to loiter. You will not be alone. Your friends will have retired, too.

No one will expect anything from you, not even military service. You can never again become unemployed. You will be invited to schoolboy get-togethers, you will be involved in marriages, your advice will be sought, and generally you will enjoy all freedoms—freedom of speech, freedom from want and worry, freedom from bad health, freedom from fear. So everybody looks forward to retirement in Turkey, the earlier the better, the more the merrier. Your gain will also be society's gain! Retirement does not mean loss of face or loss of status either at home or in the outside world. It means leisure and pleasure for the whole family, and everyone looks forward to it. Even the drop in income is an insignificant one and no one ever bothers to mention it.

There were several retired persons whom I came to know very well indeed as they lived in the same block. Some had already retired and some retired while I was in their midst. Thus, I had the opportunity to observe closely all the four stages—about to retire, retired soon after the retirement, settled down in retirement, and finally even those who had grown older in their retirement. I saw no evidence whatever of what one sees elsewhere, at least in the developing countries. Not even inflation and some decline in their own health or the health of their spouses made any difference to them. Since they did not seem to have lost anything, there was no urge to gain anything in return. They had obtained freedom for themselves, which they had always desired, and with their income after retirement and the income of their grown-up children they continued to live as a family together in a system of which they were proud and which met all their physical, psychological, emotional, and other needs.

If you wish to retire, be one with the retired ones in Istanbul.

20. Turkish Language

THE TURKISH LANGUAGE is spoken by about thirty-five million people. Though most of the Turkish people who speak Turkish reside in Turkey, Turkish is spoken also by some 250,000 persons in Yugoslavia, about 200,000 in Bulgaria, 200,000 in Greece, and more than 110,000 in Cyprus, as well as in many other parts of the world.

Ninety percent of the population of Turkey speak Turkish; 6 percent speak Kurdish. Then there are some who speak other languages too (or perhaps only)—Arabic, Circassian, Armenian, Georgian, and Laze minorities. The Bulgarians, the Russians, the Greeks, the Armenians, the Israelis, the Jews, the Druses, the Lebanese, the Syrians, the Iraqis, the Egyptians, the French, the English, the Germans, the Swedes, the Yugoslavs, the Italians and others who live in Turkey all try to speak some Turkish. And those who have a dual nationality (or hope to be nationals of Turkey at some future date) almost always speak Turkish.

At the borders, it is customary for the neighbors to speak Turkish and, therefore, the number of people who speak Turkish in the frontier areas of the U.S.S.R., Iran, Iraq, Syria, Bulgaria, Greece, Yugoslavia, and Rumania is also significant.

The Turks expect you to know the Turkish language and to learn it well, to be grammatically correct and perfect in pronunciation. If your grammar is not right, impeccably right, do not expect to be understood (not that they do not understand what you are saying). And if you are not saying it well, do not expect to be understood either (not that they do not follow your pronunciation). They simply want you to understand that to be one of them you must at least speak their Turkish language correctly. But do not feel offended: this is also what they do to their children. You will find boys and girls, even when too small to do better, being forced to pronounce correctly every single letter, word, phrase, and sentence. You must also know that correct grammar, correct syntax, correct pronunciation are still not fully correct unless the gestures that go with each word, phrase, and sentence on the one hand, and intention, circumstances, who says what to whom and when, on the other hand, are also correct.

The Turk makes an excellent Turkish language taskmaster. In any case, for me, while grammar and gestures (I had been taught to have the least to do with them) were somewhat of a problem, at least pronunciation was not, because the alphabet of my mother tongue, Sindhi, contains fifty-six letters, and what with *zer, zabar, pesh, nukte,* and their variations, there was nothing which I could not pronounce well enough to claim understanding as my reward of effort at speaking the Turkish language.

There is still one more aspect of the Turkish language that needs to be highlighted. When the Turks are in a group (that is, more than one) and especially when the group is one of women with a small scattering of men, they will continue conversation indefinitely in their own Turkish language. This conversation will completely ignore the fact known to each one of them that you are present and that you do not understand Turkish, and even the further fact that you resent this more so when it is not polite to do what they are doing. You must get reconciled to this and try to learn the Turkish language as quickly and as well as you can if you wish to be in such company (that is, if you cannot avoid it or you seek it). Do not ask for sympathy or understanding.

Then, of course, it is essential that you should know about certain Turkish words, not because these are used most frequently but because their multiple uses reveal at least a part of the Turkish character.

Yes and No

It is wonderful to be able to say yes, so they say *evet.* And when they feel like enjoying this wonderful feeling more and more, they say *evet, evet*. The more often you hear it, the better it is. But when *evet* is not said, do not assume the affirmative just because no has not been said. It could still be no even when it is not spoken. This is when you should watch. They do not like to say no or be in that position when *evet* cannot be said. It is not pleasant. It is not even dignified. When negative is the reply, it may mean that something was asked or was expected but could not be done. Well, that is decidedly unpleasant. It means sometimes even a loss of face. If there is no escape from saying no, it must be said briefly. But that too amounts to saying something that is disagreeable. There is also no gain if no is the answer.

You should observe carefully (this process should commence almost simultaneously when something is asked or is required which could possibly have a negative reply), and this you must do by looking up and down at the person to whom you are speaking or who is speaking to you. Then, suddenly, you will notice the chin going up and possibly the head too somewhat, and the eyes going to their roof and the lids remaining stuck up for a twinkle. You have had it. This was the famous no—*yok* in the written and rarely spoken Turkish language.

Once you have had *yok* or this supreme gesture, halt. Beware and do not pursue the theme. The moment will pass by, the mood will change, the situation may become different with the passage of time or the circumstance assume a different form. Then and only then, you may go round and round again until you come to your point once more. But the point must, without doubt, look different and if possible actually be different. Get many *evet*s, talk of this and that, wait for another day, and let a circle seem a triangle and a rectangle a square before you let it appear that the moment (and not the point) has come for a reply to be made, a reply which was always intended to be a pleasure because of its magnanimity and large-heartedness. Then, when it seems that the past has been forgotten (better still, that it never occurred or existed) you will find within your clasp the *evet* that you always sought.

You will have to learn to evaluate carefully, quickly, and silently the content and the implications and the possibilities of the unspoken no, the silent no. Who made the upward lift, what was the degree of the lift, was it complete or partial, even was it of the provisional, the tentative, or the final type? To whom it was made must be taken into consideration, as well as age, sex, rank, profession, and the like. When it was made would be still another factor; then, of course, the circumstances of each situation and the scene in which such a movement was made. In the case of amour, it could even be to lead you on. The silent no could also mean the desire on the part of the maker not to interrupt your flow of words. The spoken *yok* is so final; when that is not the intention, why say it? At one time it may mean disagreement, at another, rejection; sometimes, more than the spoken no. When it is made and the maker leaves you, its finality must then be assessed.

To see the beautiful way one says no in the Turkish style is truly to admire, even to fall in love! Its gentleness befits the strong Turk. Sometimes only the chin moves upward. On other occasions it may be just the eyes, only a shade though. The nose never moves with a tilt but just by itself, though the position of the lifted nose is also significant in this whole complex series of movements and in this sequence of the silent no. At other times, the eyes do not move at all and the whole act is completed between the movement of the neck and the rise and fall of the head. It is one of the most spoken movements you will ever meet.

Big

Buyuk is not only a Turkish word for big, large, or grand, but something worthwhile to be done or sought out or possessed. Whatever you do, whatever you purchase, whatever you make, even whatever you invent (even if it be a story), it must always be *buyuk*. *Buyuk* is also not to be added on as one would do in another language—more and then most. Here *buyuk* is enough.

Always think *buyuk* and do everything in a big way. Someone who ignores this or offends the concept does so at his peril!

Once I was witness to a discussion that showed complete disregard of this national character. Three or four senior international specialists from the United Nations came to Istanbul with a view to persuading the Turks to produce tomato paste in tubes for the Saudi market. The Turks agreed to it at the meeting at the Chamber of Commerce and everything was going fine when the specialists almost in chorus said that it was essential that the tomato paste should be put out in small tubes. What an offense it meant to the Turks! To be asked to produce something for someone was bad enough, but since it was for friendly Saudis it might even be welcomed, but small tubes—never. So the discussion was dropped. It would be good for everyone to remember the importance of *buyuk*.

Buyuk is not only a word or a thought, it is a reality. Off Istanbul there are several islands. One of these is called Buyuk Ada. This means "Big Island." The Buyuk Ada belongs to the Republic of Turkey, but some said that Turkey is only the owner of the island. The possession is in the hands of the Jews, the Druses, the Armenians, the Greeks, and some others. The Turks go to the island only as visitors and holiday makers. But I think that some selected Turks also own villas and houses, though only a few, and what they possess is not extensive. However, the armed services would certainly have had military installations as well as facilities of the holiday type for their members. Buyuk Ada is not only big, but it is also beautiful. A day's trip gives you much more than a day's pleasure.

The concept of *buyuk* permeates all areas of life in Istanbul. Here are some examples of my own experiences with *buyuk*.

A small bath plug attached to a chain was used to keep the water in the tub for a bath. The plug in my bathtub was an ineffective one and it was necessary to replace it, so I went to buy one. I went from shop to shop and from one quarter to another and even to specialist shops for sanitary fittings, but I could not get this small plug for the bathtub. The shops were willing to sell me the whole bathtub, a new one, which would have the plug and the chain, but there was no such small piece, all by itself, available for sale. A big shop could not sell such a small thing. Then I went to one shop whose patron I had come to know. He took pity on me and gave me the bath plug and the chain without charge because he could not show it as a sale, though he added that he would now never be able to sell the bathtub alone. This was quite a *buyuk* purchase for me.

The other episode concerned another item, the opposite of *buyuk*. I was with a friend who wanted to change his spark plugs. At the garage, the master technician asked a young apprentice to do it. How could the *Buyuk* do what the *Kucuk* ("small") could do, as the plugs were *kucuk* too? The plugs were changed, but the engine would not start. The master technician, however, would not lend a hand for such a small job, so at last when he came over he decided that it was not the plugs at fault but the engine of the car. So the car engine required *buyuk* attention.

Slowly

Yavas, yavas (slowly, slowly, by and by). Don't rush. Never be in a hurry and don't expect anything to be done at once. This is not the Turkish way. And, therefore, everyone is relaxed, at ease; life has a slow pace, good for this world and for the next one too. There will always be time if you allow it to pass slowly. It was there before and time will be there hereafter. Be cool about it. Accept the pace of events and do not overtake anyone or let anyone overtake you. Everything in its good time. There is time for everything. Life is long. Walk. At best, move. But never run. Now that you are in Turkey, do it the Turkish way. Do not even hasten the end of today, much less advance the arrival of tomorrow. Lie low in sun and warmth and swim from time to time.

Yavas means slowly. This word is spoken often and is immortalized in practice. You must learn to respect it. Having made the usual other comparisons between Turkey and other countries, some not so polite persons have even played with the beloved *yavas* of Turkey by coining a new word to bring Ankara and Washington (D.C.) closer to each other. What Washington (the government) is to the U.S.A., Ankara is to Turkey, so to make the two rhyme Ankara is also called "Yavasington."

Immediately

If *yavas, yavas* is the Turkish way of life, what was to be done (in an emergency, for example) if some speed was required? I must now tell you the lesson I learned so that you will not have to learn it. In the need to settle certain things on arrival, I found that one way of dealing with *yavas, yavas* was to find out what the Turkish word for "quickly" was. As I had no dictionary then, I asked. The word was *simdi*. To make it faster, I used to employ "*simdi, simdi*" the same as "*yavas, yavas*" was used as two words. So I would say from time to time when something needed to be done quickly, "*simdi, simdi*." But it was all the same. "*Simdi, simdi*" became the same as "*yavas, yavas*."

I began to ask for a still quicker word. It was *cabuk* and I made it "*cabuk, cabuk*," that is, "faster faster." Not a move. Then a compromise was struck. "*Yavas, yavas*" at one end. "*Cabuk, cabuk*" at the other end. In between, "*simdi, simdi*." But what worked was only "*yavas, yavas*." This was not good until I worked out something more. I made it "as *simdi* as possible." This, I am happy to say, did work, on limited occasions within emergency circumstances.

So if "immediately" is what you are after, go elsewhere, but when this is not open to you, you will be the closest to it more than anyone else if you follow the order—"*yavas, yavas*," "*simdi, simdi*," "*cabuk, cabuk*," "as *simdi* as possible," "*yavas, yavas*."

Tomorrow

Yarin ("tomorrow") is intended to convey, depending upon the circumstances in which it is used, the day that follows today, or the tomorrow following tomorrow. Generally, it means that it is not certain when it will happen or when it will be ready; it means not today definitely. But you yourself should avoid the word *yarin*, as it may mean that you do not wish to help, at least today. You must look at what lies behind, what is said, by whom it is said, to whom it is said, and why it is said.

Yarin is the *mañana* of Turkey and more!

Come

Gel means "come." The mother teaching her child to walk faces the child and endearingly calls to the child "*gel, gel*" and so encourages the child, and step by step the child learns to move forward toward the mother. But you will also hear "*gel, gel*" on another occasion, and then you must be careful, depending of course on how you are positioned. When a truck (or another vehicle of its type) has to move backward, someone stands in the center of its rear, taking a position where the driver cannot see him, and begins to call out "*gel, gel*." This means you can move backward. Depending upon the loudness of the call and the frequency of its repetition, the driver knows how much to move backward, an inch or a meter. Having moved backward the driver stops. Then "*gel, gel*" is repeated and the driver begins his backward move again. This way "*gel, gel*," goes on until the whole maneuver is completed.

Please

Lutfen means "please." But depending upon the circumstances —the gestures that go with it on any given occasion or who says it to whom and when—it could convey much more, something so typical of the Turkish character. *Lutfen* could mean please, of course. It could also mean, with appropriate gestures and when it follows or precedes the gesture—go, come, give, hold, and the like, the "please" appearing as a prefix or a suffix. It could also be used to convey "be so kind" (on making a request) or "would you" and the like. It could even become a kind of polite command or order, depending upon its context.

Even when you are not sure what you have in mind, say *lutfen!*

Please Plus

Buyurm could indicate a lot of things. While someone is offering something, it would mean "please take." While offering a seat, "please sit," "please lead," "after you." It is used in a variety of ways, special Turkish ways, situations in which even some special words or a single word follows *buyurm*. It is "please plus."

You may find a young boy, twelve or more, standing outside the door of a small restaurant or café, calling out loudly for all to hear, "*buyurm, buyurm,*" and opening and shutting the door, even if the listener is not near at hand. This is to invite you to come in because what is inside is worth eating or is special.

Buyurm was also the call of the *dolmus* barker at important centers. He would stand calling out the place of destination of different *dolmus*es and as each person approached he would open the door of the car inviting you to enter. Some did, some did not, depending upon where they were going. He kept on calling for one *dolmus* following another as these left one by one.

Sir and Madam

Efendim could follow a name. It could be *Bey Efendim*. It could be an honorific. It could mean "you," "your turn," "what do you say," a simple "please do." Again, circumstances, gestures, persons saying it, to whom he or she is saying it are important. Sometimes it could also mean agreement or consent or approval. *Efendim* could mean say it again. It could follow the name, man's or woman's. Man refers to his boss as *Efendim*. It could mean a simple "mister," too, but only when it follows a man's name. A wife refers to her husband as *Efendim*. Simply put, it means sir or madam or yes to both.

In Between

Bey could follow a name, when *Pasha* may not be appropriate (*Pasha* is much more). And when *Efendi* may not be sufficient, *Bey* is added. Sometimes both *Bey* and *Efendi* are added and it becomes *Bey Efendi*. At other times, to use *Bey* would amount to revealing one's backwardness, because *Bey* has dropped out of use in many places. *Bey* cannot be used in the case of a woman or a lady, while *Efendi* could, in appropriate circumstances, be employed when speaking to a lady.

Good-bye

When someone says good-bye or au revoir you will hear *gule, gule* in Turkey—sweet, sincere, true words of parting. It is a good-bye, a farewell, a wish and a hope of meetings in the future. It is a response to good-bye.

Another time you will hear it is when you are wearing something new, for instance. Your friends will wish you *gule, gule*—"may you enjoy it," they will say—words of praise, affection, sincerity.

The End

At the end of a book you will find *tamam*. This means "the end." As it is customary in Turkey for the same word to mean different things, *tamam* could also mean "complete," "ready," "that is right," "entire," "finished," depending upon varying situations and circumstances.

The nearest in practice to O.K. in Turkish and even more than the American O.K. is *tamam*. It may mean "enough." It may mean "agreed." It may mean "O.K." When *tamam* is said and the intention is to ascertain whether it is all agreed and understood or the other way around, there is a pause. Consent is then assumed and the matter proceeds. Sometimes *tamam* even fetches a *tamam*, the first one is a question seeking agreement and the second one is giving agreement. Sometimes *tamam* is also said to convey an offer. If a price is asked and you offer less, you say *tamam* after your offer and then you wait. Eyes meet eyes and, if the answer is in the affirmative, you will hear *tamam*. If it is not, the bargaining would have just commenced.

21. Correspondence

WE FOUND THE TURKS to be masters at the art of writing. First, never write at all. But if you have to do it, be extremely brief, so brief that you can never be misunderstood. Whatever you have to say, say it but do not put it in writing. Writing means reading, interpretation, confusion, legalities even. When you have to write, try your utmost not to have to sign. Signature is the most valuable part of you and your writing. Do not part with it. After the writing has served its purpose but you cannot tear off the whole, at least tear out the signature.

Letters and all mail at my apartment were delivered first by hand of the *kapici* and later by no hand at all. It was deposited on the seat of the waiting chairs in the entrance hall and each tenant looked for what he was looking for.

The best way to get one's mail was not at the office, as all mail was opened and seen because it was expected to be office mail, even when it was marked "Personal and Confidential." So I took a post box in my own name and there the mail remained safe except on a few occasions when there was a note that the mail had been opened by the censor and resealed. The censor was a fair authority, and he did not want to leave any room for guesswork. The correspondence that came even from government and other authorities was extremely brief, few words and few points. All clear "To Whom It May Concern." Equally, the correspondence came in envelopes that had not been closed so that no evil eye could look within on the way.

To the Turks, word of mouth, the spoken word, is more important than writing. It is perhaps more lasting among the Turks. The word of honor, once given, is always meant and kept. Every Turk learns to be a man of honor and the keeper of his word. Letters and correspondence are not for friends among friends. It is only when distance keeps you apart that you may write. Otherwise be close for a whisper and a word. Letters are for those who are not close enough.

Writing is a clerical pursuit, and a Turk will never ever be a clerk!

22. Filing

WHEN YOU HAND OVER A PRESCRIPTION at the pharmacy, the pharmacy keeps it; obviously, to file it for reference and record. But the filing the Istanbul pharmacy does is unique. There is a drawer in which all prescriptions are kept, without any indexing, punch holes, tags, dates, alphabetical or any other order. One prescription lies on top of the other, and the pile grows and grows. Even when it grows to its utmost possible height it simply overspills into another drawer, without anything being sorted out, removed, or destroyed. If the need arises to find a prescription—in order to repeat it, for instance—the whole pile is taken out, and as a result of systematic and orderly search, the required prescription is located and then acted upon. Without any nervousness, hurry, or uncertainty, the prescription is acted upon and then put back on the top of the pile. Every pharmacy is the same.

Opticians follow the same method. I had a friend to whom I went over and over again, sometimes out of fun to see how the system worked, hoping that at least once it would fail. (Do not forget that it is not the hands of one, but many who do the researching and the replacement.)

There is another aspect to this filing, too. It gives the opportunity to improve one's memory and to remember the face of every customer with his or her name.

23. Turkish Law

TURKISH LAW IS EXCELLENT in its content and practice and fairness. You will also hear about Turkish justice. These are realities. The sense of justice prevails. What gets challenged is neither justice nor the Turkish laws.

You will hear about Turkish law from the Turks all the time if they wish to threaten you, if they know that you could be threatened, or if you corner them. This is regarded as an easy, legal way to deal with the situation, particularly when legal action is neither necessary nor possible. They know very well indeed how to benefit from the Turkish law. When they do not know but are rich and can afford legal aid, they draw on it, as the number of lawyers is adequate.

Although you may have little to do with the legal system, you would find it interesting, even useful in some ways, while dealing with the Turks and appreciating their ways, to know that in Turkey there is, in practice, the Swiss Code of Civil Law and the Italian Code of Criminal Law, but when it comes to trade, business, industry, and commerce, it is the German Code of Commercial Law that prevails. These laws became Turkish laws, almost unchanged, in 1926. Among these three important legal systems and the fourth unwritten one, it is no wonder that Turkish law and Turkish justice are comprehensive, and the number of lawyers has to be large.

24. Islam

ALMOST 99 PERCENT OF THE PEOPLE of Turkey are Muslims, although Islam (the religion of the Muslims everywhere in the world) is not a state religion. I went to almost every mosque in Istanbul and at Ankara: the old ones, the ones that were converted into mosques, the new ones, and the ones still to become mosques. I went at the time of midday prayers and at times of other prayers too. I went when the tourists went. I also went when God was alone in the mosque. When the festivals began I went more often. This is what I saw—that is, what I think what I saw.

I saw that the common man was more present at the mosque and it was he who was praying the most, led by the leaders who look after the common man. The rich, the sophisticated, and the educated went to the mosque on ceremonial occasions and perhaps only then. I did not see Turkish women in any numbers at the mosques except on occasions when there were ceremonies in which they were involved—death of a relative, for instance. The other women one saw at the mosques were mostly tourists.

25. Medicines

YOU COULD GET ALMOST ANY MEDICINES you wanted in Istanbul. You would find the prices very cheap, should you compare them with prices in other Western and even Eastern cities. You will also notice that the prices are all printed on each item you buy. And as you will no doubt put in a claim for reimbursement to some insurance or social security system, as most people do in Istanbul, you will notice that the packet in which the medicine is sold has a perforated corner with the price printed on it. This is torn off the packet and fixed on the receipt and the receipt then given to you.

There is another aspect of the medical supplies that would make you feel well and happy. Most of them are made either by or in collaboration with the Swiss, the British, and the Americans—with the Swiss most important of all. And these are made in Istanbul (again mostly by the Swiss). Of late, some independent makers and some subsidiaries have appeared on the scene, but they are small. The Turkish medicines, an inheritance from the past, continue to be made exclusively by the Turks, though.

In addition to the supplies of medicine, the pharmacy facilities are excellent. These are comprehensive, located almost at your doorstep, with a trained pharmacist in charge, supported by a young boy assistant in almost every case. They are open almost always (some close-by place was always open), friendly, ready to provide first aid should you need it, almost always with someone available at the pharmacy or one who visited the pharmacy at fixed hours to give you an injection if that was also what you needed.

26. Hospitals

ISTANBUL IS THE LARGEST CITY in Turkey, and by any standards it is one of the biggest cities of the world. When you take into account its past and its present growth, you recognize the extent of the need for hospital facilities.

You will see the American hospital (set up by the Americans, though not for the Americans only, and, three or four years after my being in Turkey, run completely by the Turks). You will also be led to the German hospital. I saw this hospital while visiting an international official who would touch no other service except the German. And then I also saw the Italian hospital, as it was in charge of all our international medical examinations. I saw the French hospital, too, and was allowed by a friendly doctor to see his skill as a plastic surgeon.

But I wondered what the Turks did who were not interested in the American, the German, the Italian, and the French hospitals, and those who could not afford the treatment at these foreign-inspired and -led hospitals. So I asked and researched and found. I was, in the end, able to visit three completely Turkish hospitals: one because a meeting was held there to which I was invited, and the others because I knew a professor who worked at one of them. But these were not enough by any stretch of imagination, except of course for the fact that a Turk knew how to look after himself and did not completely admire himself if he had to be hospitalized. So the supply had not grown because the effective demand had not been high.

The situation at Ankara was different. The Haceteppe Hospital, completely Turkish, would do credit to any great city and was the pride of all of Turkey.

27. Cholera, Smallpox

CHOLERA IS QUITE A HAZARD in Turkey in more ways than one would imagine. If there is cholera or even a scare of it, the tourists do not come. This is quite serious. Therefore, cholera must be prevented. And if it occurs, it must be controlled. It must never appear to be an epidemic. Above all, the facts must never be released. If released, the scare must be held in check.

I will be specific. I went to a neighboring country on an official visit. Before leaving I checked the cholera situation in Istanbul and in the country I was visiting. I also checked about the health certificate requirements from the two airlines—one that would take me out and the other that would bring me back. And even when it had been confirmed on good authority that what I had learned was reliable, what I had found out was not enough, as you will soon see.

On the day of arrival in the neighboring country I checked again. I was told that Istanbul had changed the rules of the game. A fresh inoculation would be required when I went back to

Istanbul a few days later, because it had been announced on the radio that there was a serious outbreak of cholera in the city I was visiting. Fact or fiction at one end or both, the next morning I went and got an inoculation. And then I asked the airline to check with Istanbul to see if this would hold good. The telex reply was that although it was not necessary (it was the airline of the neighbor replying), what had been done was enough. Nevertheless, I requested my colleagues at Istanbul to meet me at the airport to see me through. But when I arrived, colleagues or no colleagues, diplomatic identity card or no card, I was coming from a city in which there was a cholera epidemic and so, along with the other passengers, I must go to the Quarantine Hospital for a quarantine of the necessary period of three to five days. The fact that I had a valid health certificate and the further fact that I had been inoculated were not facts enough. So we went to the Quarantine Hospital. There my colleagues began their well-tried methods of persuasion and intervention and the deal was made. The deal was that they would let me go on the understanding that I would stay at home (and not spread the disease beyond my own family) and would agree to return to the hospital if the situation so demanded. In the meantime they would make the necessary laboratory tests to determine whether I was free from the infection of cholera.

While cholera is of concern to the Turks, particularly to the Turks in Istanbul and the others who depend on tourism, they have no interest whatever in smallpox. Unfortunately, I had reason to concern myself with smallpox while I was at Istanbul. But this was only the small matter of my getting an endorsement on my International Health Certificate that I had been revaccinated at Istanbul. This naturally also involved getting the revaccination. Lightheartedly, therefore, I went to the Public Health Authority concerned, having taken the usual care to take along a colleague. The authority was very authoritarian. The declaration was positive, forceful, and negative. Endorsement would not be made. Revaccination would not be done. Why did I need it?

Where was I going? Where had I been before? The whole range of questions at which the Turkish bureaucracy excels.

I said I was going abroad. International health requirements compelled me to get revaccination done and to have the endorsement made on my health certificate. The tickets were produced and inspected, then the Diplomatic Identity Card issue to me by the Republic of Turkey. But to no avail. Out came my U.N. laissez-passer. This was followed by my own national passport. All this made no mark, not even a dent. Then it was time for the intervention of an intermediary. This task was undertaken by my colleague. This, with the passage of time, began to lead us somewhere. Finally the revaccination was performed and the health certificate entries made and duly stamped. But no doubt was left whatsoever that this action was against the national interest of the republic, since there was no smallpox in Istanbul (and had never been at any time since nature and man founded the Republic)!

28. Cemeteries

I VISITED PRACTICALLY EVERY CEMETERY at Istanbul. I went to see what had happened to those lying below, having spent their lives above in honor and glory.

The poor were buried by chance. Wherever there was space they were buried under it. The way they had lived was the way they ended.

In the case of the rich and the educated (a group in their own right), they (their relatives and even friends) select with the help of the professionals where they would like to be buried and in the company of whom they would like to live through eternity, this time underground. Then they buy the land of their choice in the place of their selection. They keep on buying more and more so that when the time comes and the need arises, all the tribe can be near each other, holding hands. In such enclaves, in each other's company, they plant their future abode with trees and flowers. The gardeners who serve them in other ways when alive will then continue to serve them in the hereafter. Thus, they can see what has happened and what will continue to happen even after death.

29. Armed Services

THE TURKISH PEOPLE are very proud of their armed services, 500,000 strong. The army officers (the navy and the air force included) are the elite. The fact that there is compulsory military service for everyone (excluding women) makes the armed services an integral part of Turkish society and life. A look at Ankara would show that the armed services enjoy a special position and have a special role to play. The premises built for them and occupied by them, and their location, size, and grandeur alone make this clear. The armed services are the real backbone of Turkey.

The armed services are also unique in Turkey. When the political situation became unstable and continued to be so and when Turkey was being shaken to its foundation and martial law had to be enforced, year after year, the armed services continued to push the politicians to behave themselves and to govern well and to pursue the path of democracy. Even when asked to take over, they refused to do so on every occasion—a great credit to them. Thus, they stand out unique, to be admired.

Retirement from the services takes place at an early age, and the rate of pension is high enough to enable the officers to live on their pensions if they wish to do so. Retirement with adequate pension at early age also enables them to have a second career, and indeed more and more second-career instances are emerging even at the top of the scale. Retired service officers may now be found in several key places. Many have entered the economic sector and play a managerial role creditably.

Owing to the efficient running of the armed services and for their high morale and devotion to duty, several special facilities and conveniences are provided to them which are infinitely more to be admired than the PX of the United States or the Canteen of the British Empire. Special areas are set aside for them to construct private homes—houses and apartments, a kind of reserved strategic area. Special schools provide training for their children. Army hospitals are for their exclusive use, and these are excellent in every way. Army stores serve them even after retirement. Grants and scholarships for their sons are quite liberal.

Whenever I had a seminar going, including one on family planning, and had invited the armed services to attend at least the inauguration, they did in fact send a senior representative who sat observing and listening, and always went away with all our literature. I suppose he made a further report to the officers at the top. The armed services are fully representative of the life of Turkey and come from all areas and all sectors with one exception, so I was informed. A senior Turkish services officer had to be a Turk.

30. Helicopterized

HELICOPTERS ARE USED quite frequently in Istanbul and you will see them almost every evening. I knew a friend who wanted to purchase one but could not because the helicopter was exclusively for the use of the armed services. It could not even be used as an ambulance for anyone else.

During a certain period, when Turkey moved into Cyprus or when some hunt was on, the sky looked helicopterized, though it was never so full as the least important roadway. Of course no one ever said what they were doing up in their air, and no one ever asked what they were doing when they came down. It was always assumed that a helicopter was on military or emergency duty, though sometimes it might be only routine inspection, or maintenance duty.

31. 20 — 19 = 1

SMOKERS WHO WISH TO PURSUE THEIR PLEASURE in the national interest, fundraisers, those who wish to purchase or sell arms, students of deficit financing, members of governments, political parties, the armed services, flyers of planes, mathematicians, and all those who wish to know how great the Turks are and how original and unique they have been in their approach to various matters, would be especially interested in the following press report:

50 years ago
The Ankara Parliament orders that in future all packets designed for twenty cigarettes would contain 19, the odd one becoming the property of the Turkish Government as a means of raising revenue for the construction of aeroplanes to build an airfleet for the country.

Now you know where the Turkish air force comes from and who has paid for it.

32. The Sky Is the Limit

ONCE THE VEIL IS LIFTED, the sky is the limit. This is literally true. Women in Turkey, more so in Istanbul, are free to do what they like and how they like. The veil has been lifted from their beautiful faces. When doubts are still expressed and questions asked about the freedom of women in Turkey, one instance will show the way. Once I witnessed a military show at Ankara, on the occasion of the Fiftieth Anniversary of the Republic of Turkey. In the midst of the display, beautiful colored parachutes came down from the sky in large numbers. Do you know who landed on the ground? Turkish girls. For them and for others like them, the sky is the limit!

33. Tourists

ISTANBUL IS A STAR ATTRACTION. The tourists come to see Istanbul, to see the past and to find what Istanbul has to offer. It is, therefore, essential to keep the attraction as attractive as possible and also to hold in capture the glory of the past. If the past becomes the present or the present neglects the past, Istanbul will not be what the tourists seek.

Istanbul must also be made worthwhile for those who come to buy, to sell, to spy. If tourists come to meet the Turk, make this possible. If they come to photograph, let them do as they like. If the tourists want to be invited, invite them. If they want to see, let them see; better still, show them. If they want to do the rounds or complete the circuit, assist. Give them what is wanted of you, of Istanbul, and of life in Istanbul. Don't let them down or spoil their fun or neglect them. There are others waiting to be what you have been.

Tourists do not like cholera, strikes, martial law, traffic jams, delays, poor service, indifference. Tourists do not like high prices at hotels, at shops, at terminals.

Tourists want all that Istanbul has to offer, cheap, cheap, cheap. They do not have much money and their tastes are jaded. What you cannot do or cannot give, always offer.

34. Covered Bazaar

THIS IS A MUST. I will tell you what I found and what I missed so that you can do better, although no one ever did well in the Covered Bazaar. With the atmosphere, the languages, the items for sale, the antiques, the new items, and the vast range of whatever you ask for—clothes, shoes, furniture, bedding, leather goods and garments, old watches and vases and copper and china and brass —but above all the bargaining, the haggling, the Turkish coffee, and the seductive caresses of the shopkeepers with their eyes, hands, and manners, you never got the better of anyone. There were also old guns and swords and armor, stones and gold and ornaments.

The Covered Bazaar is at least five hundred years old, perhaps even a century more. There are four thousand merchants inside the bazaar and many more on the outside. The Covered Bazaar is the place for you if you are an insider, as you will find all insiders there—from the village, from the town, from the cities, and from Istanbul. It is also the place for you if you are an outsider, for you will find all types of tourists and visitors. You will also meet buyers from the outside world looking for bargains to make bargains on return.

You can buy what you want to suit your taste and your price. You can sell, too: blue jeans, if you are a girl, preferably an American one; camera; handbag, empty or full; shoes, if the size is large; money, in any currency; overcoat, raincoat, fur coat; a watch, if it is Swiss; gold and jewels.

All languages can be spoken and understood in the Covered Bazaar. There is no better place in Istanbul if you are a spy; none better if you are looking for one. Whatever needs to be done, bought or sold, hired or exchanged could most successfully be done under the cover of the Covered Bazaar.

35. Glittering Gold

ALL IS NOT GOLD that glitters. But in Turkey, whatever glitters is gold!

When you are in the Covered Bazaar, you will come to an inside section where the whole lane is lit up and glittering. You will feel it even if you cannot see it, should you decide to walk with eyes shut, as you will feel the heat of the electric bulbs illuminating all showcases containing items made of gold. The glitter will overpower you. Every such shop has the inside lit up with naked electric bulbs. It always has displays, and these counters have gold lit up the same way.

Here you will find people standing with their arms resting over these counters, with lights underneath. They pass, once or twice, and then they stop here and there. Then they go in and out they come with gold, made-up gold which they have bought. Parting with money they have acquired wealth, eternal security, and everlasting status. People from the villages buy. People from the town and the city buy. All buy gold, all the time, the poorer they are the more gold they seek; when they can afford it, they buy it, even if it be bit by bit.

Gold makes the inheritance, the status, the wealth, the display, the security, the most outstanding mark which separates one from the other. Gold is the signboard of the shop that glows with its lights. You can see it far away. And like a moth you go to it, fascinated by the shine of desire.

Gold glitters even on glass from which you drink your wine. In Turkey gold glitters in the daytime, even when it does not reflect the sun. Those who own it feel the glitter in their hearts even when asleep. Remember that the Horn of Istanbul is the Golden Horn!

36. Cluster of Women

A CLUSTER OF WOMEN, all one's own and for one's own exclusive pleasure, kept apart, well groomed, prepared and well guarded, is what the harem is all about, is it not? Even at the university, if someone had more than his share of girlfriends, those constantly with him or around him were called his harem. You have read of the harem in books. When you thought of the sultans, you remembered them for their harems as much as for their empires. Harems appeared on the movie screens from time to time. But that was all there was to it. It remained a joke. But when I was going to Istanbul to live and work, the joke was revived.

At Istanbul I saw no evidence of any harem anywhere. No one even raised the subject. There it rested until the time came when I began to purchase presents for my friends back home on my first visit. The first thing that was suggested to me by a Turkish friend as an essential present from Istanbul was a harem ring. So I asked him about it. What was it? I had never seen anyone wearing a harem ring, had I? No, you had not but I will take you to the place where you can buy it.

So we went to the Covered Bazaar, the first place to which you go when you want to purchase a present. There he took me to the shops of glittering gold, and there it was—the harem ring. There were three main types, with three, four, and five (maximum) thin rings, almost of uniform size, held together by a small clasp. Some had blue, cheap stones. Others green. Some red. I think some also had white stones. While still others, very few ones, had a mixture of stones. These harem rings were made of nine-, fourteen-, or eighteen-carat gold. The rings were only of two or three sizes, to fit the fingers of all hands. There were none separately for men or for women; my friend would not tell me whether these were worn or bought by men or women, nor would the shopkeeper, adding that you might buy them for either or for both. They also did not tell me any historical facts about the colors or the number of rings in each ring, nor any current yarn or fantasy. As these rings were not expensive, I purchased two or three for my most manly and harem-interested friends.

The harem rings were highly appreciated, and my thoughtfulness in bringing them and my choice of colors and layers of rings in each ring received appreciative comments. These were followed, on the spot, by multiple requests to send many more on my return to Istanbul, and on my second home visit to carry enough supply to go around among not only manly men but also womanly women.

When I returned to Istanbul I began to make more inquiries about harem rings. No one was seen wearing them, men or women, although some rings did look like harem rings on coffee girls at selected hotels. At discotheques one saw harem rings being worn as playthings or as costume jewelry. But as regards any explanation about the layers of rings in a harem ring or about the colors, none was available. Who wore them or should wear them also fetched no explanation.

Now I must tell you about the real harem, though an old one, also the only real and existing one, at Istanbul. At the Topkapi Palace (where the famous Turkish Diamond lies secure and not so secure and where the band plays on ceremonial occasions in the dress and the form of the days of the sultan, and where the museum brings admirers from across the frontiers) there is a harem, closed and sealed. This has been so during the last several decades, maybe even a century or more. Suddenly its opening was taken in hand and it was being cleaned and dressed up for the occasion, a ceremonial visit from the Queen of England.

I had the opportunity to go and see it well before the opening day by the courtesy of friends. An attractive, English-speaking young Turkish lady was there to receive me and to show me around. We were taken from section to section, from one room to the other inside and out again, courtyard following courtyard. There was a running, well-briefed commentary given by our charming guide, who had been specially trained for this single most-sought-out tour. We were shown all there was to see, but we never saw any members of the harem.

37. Carpets

YOU MUST BUY A TURKISH CARPET, even if you already have a Persian carpet and an Indian carpet. If you have one Turkish carpet, buy some more. If you are not a lover of carpets, become one for the sake of the Turkish carpet. It may not be a magic carpet, but it is certainly a woolen carpet and will lie at your feet for decades and, if you care for it, even a century or two. It will remain a family heirloom.

When you are in Turkey, more so when you are in Istanbul and for any length of time, you must make it a point to see almost every kind of Turkish carpet, the leading carpet shops (this includes almost-hidden shops and their warehouses and what the owners keep for themselves and their select customers in their homes), the places where carpets are made (villages, small carpet-weaving centers, and workplaces and homes of weavers), the enterprises organized by government and by some of the banks. You must try to understand the details of quality, the design patterns, the types of weave, the knots to a square inch, the fastness of colors, the skills of the girls (sometimes very young indeed), the women, and the few men who make them. This takes time, but it is well worth it—not only to know what to buy but to appreciate what you buy.

Then you must learn to recognize their age. This will come bit by bit, the more you listen and the more you ask. The more cups of coffee you drink at different places, the more knowledge will be imparted to you, and the more discerning you will become. While on the subject of the age of carpets, I must tell you what I was told, lightly enough, but that does not mean that it may not be true. "As the stock of old carpets is getting low and as the demand is rising, we spread some of our new ones in the covered bazaar and within a week, when they have been trampled upon by thousands of feet each day, we find what decades of use and storage just about achieve in other circumstances. We take them off the floors of the bazaar, clean them and wash them and dry them and there you have our new old carpets."

Another place where carpets lie under the feet of thousands is the Blue Mosque at Istanbul or the Mevlana Shrine at Konya, for instance. But here they are not only genuinely old but almost sacred too because of the prayers done on bended knees. It is the love of old carpets and the desire for cleanliness that demands that, even in homes, you leave your outdoor footwear at the doorstep before you enter. In your search for old carpets, you must also try to cultivate some owners of carpet shops (do not spend too much time with salesmen and interpreters) as well as the buyers who roam the countryside to bring to Istanbul the best that lies in the hinterland of the country. Sometimes a carpet carried on the open back and displayed as an old piece in country bazaars may also be worth a second look. It is advisable to look at carpets that have been repaired, and it may be worthwhile to identify those who have owned them before. When it comes to colors, the faded colors have a tale to tell. Listen to their story and song.

In this, as in any other field, you will learn bit by bit, the more you move around and the more they know that you know more each time they meet you. Go again and again to the same shop, to the same person, and to the same carpet. The more you know, the more they will tell you. There is pride and, sometimes, even passionate show of it in this master's business. Go on seeing, asking, comparing, admiring, searching, and perhaps you will find what you want most. You must find out and look through what is being exported and where it is going and for whom and at what prices. But if you can see what has been sold to the "best buyer" abroad and also learn of its quality, character, and place, the exposure to such knowledge would be worthwhile. Never purchase, irrespective of all the considerations including the price and even the name, unless you can live with that carpet for your lifetime and more—each time you see it, enjoying the touch of it, the feel of it, the sight of it, and the value of it.

A carpet is regarded as a rare possession, and the longer it remains unsold the higher its price rises. I saw many carpets, over and over again, some of them, and each time the price was higher—not because money had lost its value or the demand had escalated, but because time had passed.

38. Shopping

SHOPPING IS HIGHLY REFLECTIVE of life and its character and flow. So I went into it in as thorough a way as possible. I saw almost every type of shop and its goods in every shopping street and quarter. I went to the leading shops, the Covered Bazaar, the Egyptian Bazaar, the shops within hotels, the open bazaars, the shops in marketplaces, on pavements, in lanes and by-lanes.

The more shops I saw, the more I asked myself, "Where are the Turks?" Almost every worthwhile shopowner was either a Greek, an Armenian, or a Jew, but surely not a Turk. Every time the explanation was that the Turks are not shopkeepers. While the owners were not Turks, Turks were certainly working in lower positions, as salespersons, and the numbers were increasing.

The shoes in Istanbul are among the most beautiful ones I have seen and worn: handmade, of excellent leather, latest designs, newest colors; a selection to dazzle one, new ones for every new season. Made by small shops, made by many shops—each shoe an individual art piece. Everyone comes to buy shoes at Istanbul. Even when the prices went up threefold, the shoes were still cheap and more than ever worth admiration. They were made by hand, by hands who knew their skills and had adapted them to the latest trends in fashion and material.

The embroidery is excellent. The Turks are famous for it, and Istanbul is famous among the famous ones. Shirts with their designs and color and embroidery excel your expectations. Even those that are made in villages and at the homes of the artisans are valuable. Knitted items, cheesecloth, made to measure or ready-made. Ready-made clothes in Istanbul were very nice indeed and very cheap.

Turkish greeting cards are admirable. Even the schoolchildren spend all their pocket money on them, they are so beautiful in design, color, and style. Send them to all your friends and they will know that Turkey greets them, through you. You should also see the leather binding, especially in red and gold, of the expensive books in the Turkish language. You will appreciate their wonderful printing, too. Even if you cannot read Turkish, you must buy several such books to show your respect and regard for the Turkish craftsmen who make them.

If you want glassware for the table, for wines and drinks, with gold all around artistically done, or coffee cups red with gold—anything of glass, with gold or without gold—Istanbul is the place for it. Chandeliers too, made not far from Istanbul, on the Asian side, of excellent quality and reasonable price and all made by a famous Turkish enterprise in the old Turkish tradition.

39. Food

As Sweet As Sweet Can Be

YOU WILL FIND SWEETS of all kinds—the variety is almost unlimited. These are all called *helva*, and it is only when you have been eating them over and over again that you may come to know their first name. The Turks like their sweets to be *really* sweet, not just sweet. Turkish sweets are made of the purest butter. Sometimes honey and pistachio nuts form the base. Turkish honey is sweeter than honey at other places, and when you get the Royal Honey, it is the sweetest of all.

Neither Milk nor Honey

It may not be the champagne of France or the vodka of Russia, but *raki* certainly is the national drink of Turkey. Turkish *raki* is not expensive. A Turk does not get drunk on it, nor does he take it to lose his senses and to loosen himself. He takes it because every Turk takes it and it keeps the Turks together, united. As the national drink it is taken privately and in public, on all occasions.

If you have had enough of spirits, or your spirits need something else, you still have *ayran*, which looks white and will do you a lot of good. Like *raki*, it is inexpensive, everyone drinks it at one time or another, you will find it everywhere, and it goes well with Turkish food and sport. It is yogurt with water and salt.

Layer upon Layer

Inside *borek* are flour and fat, salt and cheese, meat and spinach, nuts and fruits, and what else you will, depending upon where you buy, what you buy, why you buy, and how you want to eat.

You must not only eat *borek*—various shapes and sizes, fillings of different kinds, sweet and savory, bought ready-made and filled at home, or bought and eaten on the spot—but you must understand it. You must also watch how a *borek* on a circular tray is chopped up with the blade of an axe and served greasy and hot, almost slippery, but tasty if you know how to enjoy it and eat it while you stand.

Borek is, above all, layer upon layer, just as Istanbul is a series of layers. *Borek* is a way of life.

It Is All the Same

Kebab (now internationally known and recognized) is more or less the same wherever you eat it in Turkey and by whatever name it is called: *Donner Kebab, Sis Kebab, Istanbul Kebab, Adana Kebab, Bursa Kebab, Konya Kebab, Tandir Kebab, Talash Kebab, Yogurtlu Kebab.* The name changes with the place, as you may have guessed. The name also changes with some of the main ingredients. Sometimes it changes with the type and extent of the spices added; in some cases, whether it is fried or baked, and whether baked under or above ground. In the most special case, when the *kebab* is called the *Donner Kebab*, it is slices of meat stuck, layer upon layer, on a revolving cylinder, which are once again sliced when the meat is hot and the fat dripping, the thinner the better, and served to you as the unique Turkish *kebab*.

It is the distinguished maker of *kebab*, the *kebabi*, who alone can give you the best *kebab*. Each city, and within each city every famous area, has a famous *kebabi*. You will also find it worth your while to learn to distinguish and enjoy a close companion of *kebab*, the *kofte* of Turkey—smaller minced (meat but even fish and potatoes or vegetables on occasion) food rolled up into balls: tasty and delicious.

Not by Bread Alone

We lived by bread alone from time to time, for fun and pleasure, but this was possible and enjoyable only because it was the bread of Istanbul. Turkish bread is tasy, nutritious, crisp, fresh, inviting. Try the bread without salt, butter, cheese, or sugar and even water.

Life Is Meze

Turkish *meze* reveals a great deal of the Turkish character. *Meze* is translated to mean a kind of hors d'oeuvre, but it is not. It can be large or small. It can be several fried items, many raw items, meats and cheese and salad and pickles and sweets, fish and fowl.

When you order *meze*, you never know what will arrive. It depends upon the price, the area, the kind of place, the season, the time of day. *Meze* never puts in its appearance for breakfast, as the Turkish breakfast, like the English breakfast, has a standard pattern in which there is no place for *meze*. *Meze* depends upon the intentions of the chef and the patron. It is all a surprise, though not a choice.

Smile at the surprises that it produces. Look upon the variety as a variety in Turkish life. When it is more than usual, think of the regions, the towns, the areas, and the cultures it represents. When it is hot and sweet and cold, all at the same time, think of the Turk who can take everything in stride. Each time if something new is offered, this is what you should expect in Turkey.

With a Turkish friend I went to a well-known restaurant in the best part of the Bosphorus on the European side. The object was to lay out a special dinner for a special friend from New York. Naturally, the further real object behind this personal preparatory visit was to fix not only the menu, but the menu of the *meze*. This is how the effort went. We met the patron, the floor manager,

and the chef, and by the time the discussion had generated sufficient warmth, advice was sought from some senior waiters by the
group leaders.

"What kind of *meze* do you want?"
"Whatever you suggest, but it must be the very best that you can
set up for my friend, who is coming over from New York."
"How much are you prepared to pay?"
"Price is no consideration at all."
"What about shrimps?"
"Excellent."
"Then what about mussels? This is the season."
"Excellent."
"But you must not have both."
"Whatever you prefer."
"Will fried do?"
"Excellent."
"But baked would be better."
"As you say."
"And cheese?"
"You know best."
"I think fried with flour would be ideal."
"Certainly."

Before going further, let the end be told about this *meze*. When
we sat to eat at the appointed time and on the designated date,
while there was elaborate *meze*, there were neither shrimps nor
mussels in any shape or form, fried or baked, cheese or no cheese,
flour or no flour. What was offered was not discussed. What was
discussed was offered as a part of the main meal. All said and
done, every major and minor branch of the *meze* family was
served, from raw to boiled, fried, baked, hashed, cooked, torn
apart. The whole meal was a *meze*!

Sometimes the *meze* could be a side-plate collection only. At
other times—one item following another, one hot fried crispy
leading another, it could go on and on, depending also of course

upon the flow of *raki*. Each hostess likes to add her own special item, learned from the grandmother's time. Some make varieties never heard of before.

Flats, triangles, balls, beads, rounds, and squares—all shapes make their appearance in a *meze*. In between, face to face, layer upon layer, on top and on the side, visible and invisible. On sticks and without sticks. Large, small, and insignificant. Salty, spicy, sweet, sour, hot on the tongue, meaty, fishy, all kinds of tastes and flavors. When we thought we had listed at least seventy or eighty different items belonging to various species, we had to update the figure as time passed.

Turkey is known for its nuts. This includes, in particular, the hazelnut. You could bank on all the varieties being included in the *meze*—salted, spiced, fresh. The same was true when it came to do all one could with fresh corn or the large variety of flours that are available in Istanbul. Even the crumbs were put to good use. Bread of different shapes and designs and sizes, toasted, fresh, with pastes and butter, too. Onions and garlic turned out in good form and shape. Meats and fish baked in deep earthen pits, sometimes with Turkish village bread too. Meats and fish dried in the sun, as well.

Another quality of *meze* was that one took what one liked as it was offered without any metal implements. You took it all, in one piece, and put it into your mouth.

With lamb's milk, they knew not only what to do with cheeses but also with creams. All these appeared in a variety of inner and outer forms in the *meze*. Salads, green and not so green, of all colors that could be found in any world vegetable market, including what could be imported—all went into the rich man's *meze*. Yogurts and what they add to taste was all yours to taste in the *meze*. What the Turks do with the fermented dough should excite the envy of others. On special occasions the *Donner Kebab* also appeared as a part of the *meze*. With times changing and such difficulties as the polluted fish, a lot of initiative, improvisation, adaptation, and inventiveness went into the range and the contents of the *meze*. But whatever went into the *meze* was almost always fresh and to a great extent homemade.

Istanbul has some species of birds. These came to you, if your host was of the hunting type. Some game also made its appearance from time to time. But of course there were always several preparations of the most envied chicken and its eggs. Anything salty, savory, buttery, light, and airy made its debut in one form or another. Even the heavy potatoes, turned into mini world globes, came hot and sizzling to please your palate when there was appetite no more. Spinach *kebabs* are a special delight when offered as a *meze*.

Meze is always different, always attractive, always full of variety and uniqueness. Life itself is a *meze*.

40. Coffee Houses

DON'T THINK of Turkish coffee houses as you would think of cafés. Coffee houses are much more. Generally they are run by a life's veteran; when you come to know him you will also come to know his name. That is, the name by which the coffee house is known, not called. You will get the best Turkish coffee and every time it is served, it is fresh, brought to you by a young boy, who also brings you a glass of water. One sip of coffee is followed by one sip of water, hot then cold, and when the coffee is almost gone, you chase it with all the water you can. In a coffee house you should not ask for anything else—it is there only to serve you coffee.

The greatest reason to go to the coffee house is to talk. Every

Turk likes to talk (no generalizations are intended), and at the coffee house you will find a captive audience—like the captive waters of Turkey. Everyone talks, everyone listens. And when you talk you reveal as little as you like. You argue and discuss. But even when you have no views to advance and wish to convert no one and even when you have no enemy to rival or friend to make, you may go there to talk. It does not matter who says what to whom. Everyone says to one another anything he wishes to say. No offense meant, no voices raised, no swords crossed. Just plain, simple, pleasing talk, and it is such a pleasure to listen to a Turk speaking Turkish. So you must go to the coffee house, as I went so often—to listen, to understand, to appreciate, and to observe.

Even after Islam ceased to be the state religion, the coffee house continues to be the seminary of Turkey.

As Turkish coffee is served not only in coffee houses but everywhere in Turkey and in several places outside Turkey, it may be worthwhile to say a little more about Turkish coffee. When Turkish coffee was offered, you would always be asked how you wanted it. You would be asked if you wanted it *sekar* (with sugar; if you said yes, it was always more of sugar than anyone could ever ask for). If you said *sada* (no sugar at all), it was to your taste (if you like coffee with sediment and also wish it to be bitter). But if you said *orta*, it was coffee with some sugar (that is, medium sweet). So most times one asked for *orta*.

Whenever your choice of a hot drink was being ascertained (whether in coffee houses, tea houses, or elsewhere in Turkey), you were always asked whether you would have Turkish coffee or tea. Tea was alone, all on its own. When they offer you tea they very rarely add the prefix Turkish. It seems as if Turkish coffee is a concept or a part of the Turkish way of life, while tea is only a relative, perhaps a near-relative but no more. Or perhaps it is because in Turkey it is the Turkish coffee that is read to forecast your future and to tell you of your love affairs and enemies and riches (they hardly comment on your character); and that is why

Turkish tea would be inappropriate, since tea leaves mean nothing to the Turks.

There are certain special characteristics about tea which need to be mentioned: no teapot, no milk jug, no sugar bowl, no tea strainer, no fuss. If you don't like it, don't ask for tea. The tea is brewed the same way everywhere in Turkey. It is always ready to drink. Moreover, one vessel does not replace another with fresh leaves, but the same container keeps on the boil all the time, brewing the same leaves to serve you better and better as times goes by. Then comes the most spectacular part of it. The tea is served in a small special glass which is standard throughout Turkey—as standard as the Turkish lira. Sometimes the glass has a gold border, though most of the time it is a plain glass.

The Turks, being fond of standing erect, they always serve tea in this glass with a teaspoon (more like the coffee spoon elsewhere) standing erect, alone inside the glass, immersed in tea. The spoon is intended to help you to stir the lumps of sugar, but it is up to you how to sip your tea with the spoon not spilling what you are taking or falling into your lap or bending sideways. The spoon must not be taken out, and even after the tea has been completed it must be left inside, standing erect as it was when it first reached you. Lastly, the tea is not only served in this glass but there is usually no saucer on which the glass is placed.

You are never asked how you want your tea—light or medium, for instance. It is always served the same. You also are not asked how much sugar you want. The glass arrives with the spoon in the glass, the glass standing erect (it has to) on the saucer (if there is one) with two cubes of sugar on the saucer, mostly two cubes with every glass. Tea is never served with milk. You cannot have milk with Turkish coffee, either. Turkish coffee is never served in a glass; tea is never served in a cup.

There is always someone engaged for serving tea or coffee wherever you work. If the place is small, the service comes from a neighboring place, but if it is of any size worth the mention, there is a man for it on the premises. The man brings it on a tray and serves you where you are; on a chair if there is no table, and on the table if you have no chair. As soon as you finish, the empties are whisked away quickly, even if you are in the midst of a discussion with a group—business or friendly, he could not care less. The empties must not be seen. That is the extreme sense of cleanliness which the Turk presents always.

41. Turkish Belly Dancers

I DID NOT SEE any extraordinary Turkish belly dancers though Turkey, and therefore Istanbul, was reputed to be well known for its belly dancers. But when I went to my home country for a short holiday, after about six months' stay at Istanbul, my friends asked me about the Turkish belly dancers. When I said that I had not seen any, they began to laugh at me. "You are coming from Istanbul and you have not seen the Turkish belly dancers. Very well, we will then show them to you here, tonight." So in the evening they took me to the well-advertised belly dancers from Istanbul.

The dancers in Istanbul were not so beautiful—as my subsequent inquiries, on return, showed. It was only the ones who went abroad who were the real beauties (collected from all over Turkey). But even those who were left in Istanbul were increasingly brought under the Turkish standards of morality, and the day may come when the Turkish bellies will dance less furiously and less openly and even less seductively, though certainly the Turkish belly dancers will dance always, even in Istanbul.

42. Turkish Singers

THE POWER OF THEIR VOICES, rich and compelling, the words of their songs, and the movements of their emotion hold you spellbound. When you understand the themes of their inspiration you know how deeply moved they themselves are, to move you so completely in turn. Hear them sing over the TV, the radio, and the circling disks, but there is nothing so entrancing as seeing them sing to you over dinner and over lunch at famous places in Istanbul. That is where the stars are and that is why you go to eat there.

43. Over the Shoulder

WATER IS VERY IMPORTANT in Turkey. It gives security and success. But you must also know about one other use of water in Turkey that continues to be in vogue. Whenever I was leaving on a mission, my colleagues would come out to see me off at the door and then one of them would throw water over my shoulder so as to land right in front of me. I would then walk over the water on my way out. This was to ensure my safe return and the success of my mission. So be grateful if someone throws water over your shoulder, even if you are not a Turk. Water ahead is a good sign of life ahead.

44. Population

ACCORDING TO SOME ESTIMATES the population in Turkey is increasing at about 3 percent a year. Some would like to see this rate reduced, as the rise is the highest among the least rich (another way of calling them poor), in least developed parts of the country, and in remote areas dependent on agriculture and cattle raising (grazing too). They would also like to see the rate reduced because this would make Turkey and its policy makers appear to be moving with the times. There are, however, others who believe that Turkey could easily afford to have more Turks within the country and abroad, that more Turks are a contribution to the growth and development of Islam, and that with what may lie ahead it is best to have most of everything.

Between these attitudes, the population of Turkey continues to grow. There is, however, some concern (the Turks are never anxious) at the increase in numbers at Istanbul, perhaps at Ankara, and sometimes even at Izmir. This concern is caused not because of the increase of childbirth in or out of wedlock, but because of the people moving into these three principal cities of Turkey from other centers of population, mainly villages and other areas not so prosperous. Such a movement might eventually come to be curtailed when it impinges upon the standard of living of those who live so well in the cities, but that may be a matter for the distant future.

Taking into account the total resources of Turkey and Turkey's needs for the future, the population of Turkey was not excessively large, even if the rate of birth was above the desirable objective. But certain aspects of life in Turkey made it seem necessary that the birth rate should be encouraged to come down, though some people thought that it would be best to ensure this downward trend only for the least and the less blessed. It was also argued that to make rapid industrialization possible, population was not a great help; newer technology might be the best. Again, in order to raise living standards it would be a help if population growth was controlled. There were some, however, who realized the true needs of an Islamic state, even of the Turkish kind, and did not wish to come to grips with the population of Turkey. They said it was not a problem.

45. Squatters

THE SQUATTERS OF ANKARA are famous. Everyone sees them while driving from the airport to the town. You see their huts on the right-hand side on hilltops. They stand on slopes, poor in their majesty, without water and electricity. As you move closer you will also find shanties.

More than 50 percent of Ankara's 1.8 million people live in such homes—that is as if one-fourth of the population of Istanbul lived thus. These homes are built almost overnight by the villager moving into town, alone or with the help of friends. When some vacant land is located in the midst of other squatters, the walls are erected first, and while the squatters are living in their midst, the roof is built. So the squatter, a villager from the village, now settles, perhaps for life, into another village, into a Squatter's Village.

But there are no squatters' villages, squatters, shantytowns, or quickly built huts in Istanbul. There are no vacant plots of land on which anything could be built overnight. Even though there are hilltops, these are without open spaces. There are no slopes on which you could build, either. Instead, in Istanbul you find honeycombs, beehives, spiders' webs and cobwebs, fissures and chasms, and even slums in which all the poor of the city live, not just the villagers who come lured by what Istanbul has to offer. But there are no squatters. So I thought until I was put right.

A high-level dignitary came to Istanbul from New York, an international civil servant from the United Nations. As he was the senior civil servant of his level who had ever come to Istanbul on the mission of his choice, I accompanied him to the Town Planning Authority at Istanbul. There we discussed various matters and then came to the subject of squatters.

The Town Planning Authority representative went blue in the face when we said that there seemed to be no squatters in Istanbul. He said that there were squatters in Istanbul, the biggest amount in Turkey, though totally different from the squatters of Ankara. These squatters were the richest in the city and were the biggest beneficiaries of the broken laws of Turkey. These were the men of wealth who owned the waterfront of the Bosphorus, from the Dolmabachi Palace to Kucuk Bebek, and beyond, on the front line with houses and villas and now even blocks of apartments. They had built on what they had and also built on what they did not have. They had built without approved plan, they had thrown overboard all considerations of city planning. They had done what they wanted to do and there was no one to stand in their way. These were the permanent squatters of Istanbul with water laid on, electricity, and all facilities of life.

Seeing what they had done and gotten away with, others, some more rich, some less rich, but rich in any case, had built a second line of offense against town planning and had built more and more at the back of what stood on the front. This disregard of law and regard for oneself had now spread widely into the city, and everyone was building where he liked, how he liked, and what he liked. Some kind of token approval was obtained for token construction, but that was all.

The rich and their builders had taken over the city (I saw this too in the area in whch I lived) and there was nothing that could be done about it. The rich are all-powerful everywhere, but more so in Istanbul than elsewhere. Then the Town Planning Authority representative went so far as to ask one of his deputies to take us around and show us the squatters of Istanbul. We saw what we had been told. We also saw the known slums and the beehives. So there you are. Each city has to bear its burden.

Then back we came to the town planner to ask where the newcomer lives, if he is poor. He lives one upon the other, with others like himself. That is why Istanbul needs the town planner with laws that are obeyed, with principles that are written. Istanbul has no future if the future will not conform to the past, but Istanbul must also make its own future.

46. Slums

MOST CITIES HAVE SLUMS, some through inheritance and some by acquisition. Istanbul has both: the newest slums are in the newest parts of Istanbul and consist of mostly new structures. These are the new and not-so-new blocks of modern apartments built quickly on every extra centimeter of land in the new parts of Istanbul. Blocks are built face to face, neck to neck, front to front, side to side, back to back, and up and up. While these are built quickly, they take time to be furnished and occupied.

In due course the earthen roads that lie in between and surrounding them will become roads of pride, but until then they are the dustbins of Istanbul. Also in due course, water will be laid on, electricity will not fail, the lifts will work, telephones will ring, but until then it is a frontier experience for the newcomer.

But the people want to occupy them, it confers status, the value rises, and the movement flows from the old type of slum into this newest type of slum.

47. What Do You Want to Do?

I ASKED EVERY FRIEND, acquaintance, and even those I met briefly —boys and girls, men and women, students and their parents. The question was, What do you want to do? What do you want to be? In the case of the parents the question was, What are your plans for your son or daughter? What would you like your son or daughter to do? What do you think your son or daughter would like to do? What are the plans for further study?

Before dealing with the replies, it is best to say at the start that every father had been in the army (air force or navy). Some sons were doing the military service or had just finished it and the other sons of soil would do their military service at a future date. In almost every case the mother had little to say (in their case, very limited exceptions apart, they had little to do in any case with the outside world, and the number of them who had been to the university was limited). So the sons and daughters themselves and their father, and in certain limited cases the grown-up employed brothers and the married sisters, had an influence on this decision.

The answer made by every girl was: I want to get married within two or three years after completion of studies (school or university, as was the case), and during the two or three years I would like to do some work. What work? In some shop, in some office. It never went beyond this.

As regards their fathers, every single father said that he wanted his daughter to marry well. If there was some waiting period involved, he would like his daughter to do some work. It seldom went beyond that. I came across one exception, though, in which the daughter said that she wanted to be a doctor and the father said that he would like his daughter to be a doctor as that was what she wanted. At that time the girl was still in school. As regards the pursuit of studies and the selection of subjects for study, neither the fathers nor the girls showed any particular keenness for any special subjects. The inevitable conclusion was that all concerned were keen to achieve the principal objective— a good marriage, and the sooner the better.

Not one of the sons of the rich or the educated said (whether he was at the school or at the university, and even after he had returned from army service) that he wanted to join the armed services. This was most strange because of the high esteem in which the services are held, the excellent pay and conditions of service, the facilities for retirement, the retirement benefits, the scope for promotions, the role played by the services in the past, and the present tradition of the country. Nor did a single father say that he wanted his son to join the services (even in the particular case when the father was a retired army general). This was also contrary to all expectations.

Not a single son (or a single father) even mentioned that he wanted to join the state administrative services. In one case the foreign service was mentioned, but later, on realization that foreign service meant service abroad, this too was dropped. No mention of any particular career, profession, or job was made by either the son or the father, with the single exception of the legal profession. The closest mention that came to be made in the later years of my stay was, "I would like to be an engineer," and "I want to be a manager," as if a word had gone 'round. No greater precision was forthcoming. What was wanted was employment— employment as a manager, employment as an engineer, employment of any kind; naturally, with good pay and prospects.

When it came to selection of studies, the situation was precisely the same: no strong choices, no great studies, no complex courses, no particular preferences. If pressed, mention was made of the law degree, the engineering degree, the medical degree, but all mainly with a view to finding employment. Study courses did not seem to be a matter of any particular concern or anxiety. Examinations did not strike their hearts with fear, and it was quite common to be told after the results were out: "Oh, I failed in five subjects" (if it was at the school level), or "I will do three subjects again," or "I will get my degree after three months or six months as I have to complete some parts of a course." No feeling of anything lost or anything not done well. Everyone knew the rules of the game and accepted them in the Turkish spirit.

The enlightened ones (this includes their parents), the well motivated and the bright, of course, go abroad for studies—to England, the United States, Germany, France, or Switzerland. They go on their own or on the scholarships offered by the state and by some leading enterprises. Unfortunately, it is extremely rare for a woman to show that she too deserves to go abroad and that she too is bright and well motivated.

48. University Scene

AT ONE END stands the everlasting Roberts College (the Americans claim it as their own even after it has become the Bosphorus University, and for good reasons) and at the other end is the Middle East Technical University at Ankara (although they do not make the same claim, Americans have had much to do with it). Roberts College is much smaller but more profoundly on the side of liberal arts, while the Middle East Technical University is not only much larger, about 10,000 students, but it is really a part of the Middle East. More important, it is also a true technical institution with its keen eye on politics, economics, and technical theory and practice. In between stands the University of Istanbul (founded in 1453 and completely reorganized in 1933) with its technical part akin to the Technical University and its other parts facing the Bosphorus.

At Roberts College, where I went often, both the students and the faculty had to look after themselves, and they do this well. Well fed, well clothed, well met, well housed, and if you wish well educated, the girls like to get married and the boys like to play, even to fool a little bit, and when no more is possible, to get married too. Everything else comes later.

But in the case of the Technical Department of Istanbul and the Technical University at Ankara, the concerns are much wider and the conflicts much deeper. The education platform is the arena of play for life's stakes. There it does not matter if education comes last, if first things come first. There Turkey comes first and the Turk thereafter. Education is only a small part of life, a preparation which calls for practice on a much larger campus. The students stand divided on all issues—what to study, who should teach what, who should lead whom. But these are matters of minor significance.

The most important subject for action is the present of Turkey and the possible future for all Turks. Each group wishes to be the sole architect, it being a matter of less consequence who will then live where and do what. In this determination, examinations, studies, semesters, and even years seem insignificant. A few semesters off are an investment in the future. In this pursuit of what they want, they have supporters, opponents, well-wishers, and even schemers and agitators (some say professionals too).

That is the university scene, of which student unrest is an integral and lasting part. If one fails, one can always pass later, but if one loses, all is lost.

Student Unrest

I had many friends among students. Some were living in the apartment blocks which became a big part of my life and study during my stay in Turkey. Others were their friends. I also made friends with students who came to play basketball opposite where I lived. Some more lived across the street. In some cases I made friends with students who came to our office to do research and to ask questions. I also visited each of the colleges and their various wings and campuses. Sometimes I went to listen to selected speakers. I visited students, their friends, and their places of living and study in both Istanbul and Ankara. I enjoyed the company of my student friends, and I traveled with them in the *dolmus*, on the bus, on the ferry boats, went with them shopping and to the movies and to art galleries.

During almost my entire period of stay there was student unrest—active, dormant, lying low, furious, violent, continuous, and in spells. Student unrest was a part of life. It became apparent as time went by and as friendships grew and widened that the students would never explain what the reasons for the student unrest were. They invited you to see for yourself.

The student unrest was not for academic reasons or for reasons related to studies—except insofar as the location of the campuses, the residential accommodation provided, and the level of studies made student unrest possible, easy, and convenient. It was not caused by fear of failure at the examinations, the cost of studies, or difficulty of admission. The type and level of studies provided and the quality of the faculty, the way the universities were run or the campuses administered were not factors. It was not a reaction against parental authority. The fathers knew their offspring very well indeed; they had been the same themselves, and the times had not changed. It was not because the students did not have enough to live on: they knew how to get by. Extracurricular facilities and concessions were not lacking. There was no work over the weekends and the holidays were plentiful. Not many books were needed and the pressure to study was not great. Homework figured little. Even the prospect of unemployment did not strike any fear at all in the hearts of the Turkish students. It was not against the rise in prices or the fear of compulsory military service. It was not the type of student unrest one met elsewhere and for reasons which are well established. It was student unrest in the Turkish tradition, for reasons best developed in Turkey. It was student unrest, among students: violent, with knives and pistols, blood and death, fighting in the student arena.

It was political unrest—students on the left fighting with students on the right, political parties standing at the threshold of these fights. From time to time some accounts would include groups of reasons—social and economic reasons. But in truth, it was always a case of a political fight started by the students and continued by the students with one single purpose: to beat the left or to beat the right. Depending upon which political party had the prime ministership, the fight would swing in intensity.

Every political matter was a matter of deep concern to the students, not only the future or the present of this or that party. When the number of parties grew, this only meant that the concern of the students grew with them. Thus, whether there was one or more political parties or even when there was no effective political party—as, for instance, when the martial law was in force—political matters continued to be the principal concern of students. The political parties supported them, welcomed them, but did not shed blood for them as the students did for the political parties. The students knew this, their parents knew it, government (and martial law authority) knew it, the faculty was aware of it. In the past, the students in Turkey have brought down governments and toppled parties. They will surely do the same in future.

Examinations

Examinations generally, at least in developing countries, cause tension, a psychological condition, complexes, frustration, anger, disappointment, and distress. In Istanbul that was not the case. When examination time approached, there was student unrest at the university and so the examinations were postponed, not once but often.

But when exams did take place at the school and at the university, partly because the assessment standards were reportedly not high, most students passed. For those who did not pass, the loss of face that happens elsewhere did not happen here, for two reasons. The first reason was that the numbers so involved were not small, to say the least, so what happened to one happened to many more. The parents accepted it and the students did not dislike it.

The second reason was that failures led to evening courses, and evening courses led to meeting one's friends (this may not have been as convenient when the schools were shut). These meetings were in the evenings. If one failed in one, two, three, or even six subjects, it was not obligatory to pass all of them at one time. One success followed another, and eventually all exams were passed. The evening courses continued over many evenings and for several months. No one felt shy of announcing, though not boastfully, that he or she had taken up evening courses. What this meant was understood by all concerned.

In this Turkish way, the psychological condition that examinations cause elsewhere did nothing of the kind in Istanbul. Those who passed and those who passed at some future scattered dates were all in the same category of success. Failures were never mentioned.

49. Employment

THERE IS NOT ENOUGH EMPLOYMENT in Turkey for the educated youth, particularly in the fields in which the youth would like to go. There is also not enough employment for others—new entrants, returned and retired workers, and others who transfer their jobs or have to move from one place to another. This has been the case for some years now. It is difficult to create new employment in most countries. Such has been the case in Turkey.

This situation was easy to foresee. Why then was not action taken, early enough, continuously, commensurate with the size of the problem? To do so would have required the admission that the problem existed, that it was a serious one, and that what was being done and what had been planned were not enough. No one was prepared to do so.

About 20 percent (and perhaps much more) of the labor force was jobless at one time, and about 700,000 Turks who were working in Europe had returned home—without work. Apart from the general rate of unemployment and underemployment, it is the situation at Istanbul (at Ankara and at Izmir too) which needs the most urgent attention, since urban unemployment could become the most effective agent of discontent and disruption.

50. *Bankasi*

ON OUR ENTRY INTO TURKEY, having spent the night at a hotel on the Turkish side of the frontier at Ederne—that is, on the European side of Turkey—our desire the next morning was to keep going. But already certain things stood out which raised questions. One was the number of Mercedes cars. It was almost a Mercedes car park, in which it was difficult to find my own Mercedes. The second was the number of large signboards on which the letters of the largest size were "*Bankasi*" and "Million" ("Million" was followed by some numerals). By the look of it, most of the Mercedes owners seemed to be Turks. Without knowing a word of Turkish at the time, we wondered what could possibly be the meaning of the word "*Bankasi*." Since the word "Million" also appeared, we concluded that the word "bank" had been extended and the application of "asi" at its end perhaps made no difference.

As we drove further into Turkey, these signboards continued to appear frequently, even when there were no villages, junctions, traffic centers, or people around. The boards could be seen only by those who were driving toward Turkey as they were on only one side of the road. So the banks were introducing themselves to those going into Turkey, hardly giving them the opportunity to see anything else or to think of matters other than millions.

As we intended to enjoy the Sea of Marmara as an introduction to our stay in Turkey, we stayed at a motel about three hours' drive from Istanbul for two nights. The motel had a beautiful beach, and we had a wonderful time there. Looking around at other guests, we found that they were mostly Germans (the patron was German by origin and his wife, though Turkish, spoke German), one French family, and a few Turks (mostly honeymooners). We also saw, close by, another large holiday complex (we were to see several more later on our way to Istanbul). On inquiry, we were told that the complex was owned and run by a group of *bankasi* for their employees.

Soon after arrival at Istanbul, I wanted to open a bank account and to have a checkbook. Some reluctance was shown at the idea of opening a bank account by my well-wisher friends. But in the end, after about three weeks, I had a bank account and a checkbook. The first check that I issued was for the rent of my apartment. I made it payable to the representative of the landlord. The representative protested at being given a check and would not accept it. Was it because I did not trust him that I wanted to pay rent by check? After all, he had trusted me with the apartment, a far more valuable real property. Finally, in the end, after intervention and persuasion by others, the check was accepted.

That was virtually the end of my use of the checkbook. I issued only one check for the amount of the rent each month. Consequently, I also deposited each month only the amount of the rent. I learned by talking to several friends that in spite of the branches of banks almost at one's doorstep (three branches came to be opened within the circumference of the area in which I lived, each at walking distance of three minutes from each other), it was not the practice either to put money into the bank or (therefore) to take money out of the bank, much less to receive a check or to issue a check; unless, of course, there were business reasons for doing so or unless one had several millions, some of which could well be entrusted to the banking system. It seemed that this was the true reflection of the situation, though very surprising indeed, because it seemed that the rate of interest was quite attractive.

I had one or two rather unusual experiences at the bank (the Ottoman Bank founded in 1863). This bank was a special bank dealing with foreign currency and foreigners. I asked my Swiss bank at Geneva to send me a certain amount of Swiss francs, payable to me as Swiss francs. This they duly did and charged me for their services. When I went to collect the Swiss francs I was, however, given Turkish liras and not the Swiss francs I had arranged to receive. No explanation was given. When I insisted I was, in the end, offered Swiss francs: not the amount which I was to receive, but far less. No explanation was given. So I went to see the manager. He opened my eyes. He said that if I wanted Turkish liras, I would be given the amount of Swiss francs which had been received by the bank to pay to me multiplied by the official rate of so many Turkish liras to one Swiss franc. But if I insisted on collecting the Swiss francs which the bank had received on my behalf and accepted to pay as Swiss francs (all commissions and other elements likely to be involved in the transfer had already been paid by the Swiss bank to the Ottoman Bank and repaid by me), the amount would be far less. The transaction would run as follows.

The Swiss francs would first be converted into Turkish liras (this would be the same amount as already offered to me if I would accept Turkish liras). The Turkish liras thus arrived at would then be converted into Swiss francs at the rate for the purchase of Swiss francs plus a certain commission for such a transaction. Finally, the Swiss francs so purchased would be given to me. If the Swiss francs given were far less than the Swiss francs which they had received for payment to me, it was not a relevant matter for the Ottoman Bank. I, naturally, thanked the manager and asked him to return my Swiss francs to my bank at Geneva. This he said he would do as a special favor to me.

The other personal experience was in connection with the payment to be made to the transport agent through whom I had imported a car. When I went to pay him, accompanied by a colleague (this is a must, you may have gathered), he asked me to give him a certain amount in Turkish liras. This I took out and gave him. But he would not take it, saying that I had misunderstood. He wanted U.S. dollars, again a certain amount presumably equal to the amount of Turkish liras which he had first mentioned. On double-checking with him and with my colleague that it was now U.S. dollars which were required, I went home and got them (since I always kept several currencies handy while in Turkey) and returned to the transport agent.

This time he again refused to receive the payment, though what was being offered was exactly the amount he wanted in U.S. dollars. Then came the explanation. He said that I should go to the Ottoman Bank, which was in the next street, change the U.S. dollars into Turkish liras, and bring to him the Turkish liras which he would then accept. I triple-checked with him and with my colleague about the facts of the new demand and we then both went to the Ottoman Bank and made the conversion of U.S. dollars into Turkish liras and quickly returned to the transport agent.

But acceptance did not follow this presentation either. The transport agent, in addition to the Turkish liras just produced, also wanted proof of the physical conversion. This was provided, since the bank counter girl had kindly given me a slip showing the rate of conversion, the amount converted, and the Turkish liras given. This he examined critically, but once again refused the offer. He said that what he wanted was a certificate from the Ottoman Bank that so many U.S. dollars had been converted by me for the purpose of making a payment to the transport agent so as to pay him for the transportation charges incurred, etc. Back we went to the bank and the girl confirmed that such a certificate was essential. She made out the certificate and we returned to the transport agent. The payment supported by the certificate was accepted and part of the transaction was thus completed.

When I came to know the senior ones of the senior banks, they explained that the *bankasi* holiday complexes had been set up in order to attract suitable staff, to reduce turnover of staff, to make holidays cheap for the staff, to democratize holiday taking (as the seniors and the juniors all went to the same complex), to increase the level of fringe benefits, to keep salaries from rising (less payment of income tax, which was appreciated by all concerned), and to build up an image for the *bankasi*.

As regards savings, it was generally agreed that the picture was not a rosy one. The picture was also not a rosy one when it came to investments. But the receipt of foreign currency on transfer (savings of Turkish workers abroad) was quite a substantial amount. The number of workers was large, the savings were considerable, transfers were monthly or at other intervals, and the final transfers were of large sums. It seemed that the Turkish workers too could not hold foreign currencies abroad. So there was roaring business for certain banks. In any case, the country as a whole was a beneficiary. No one, however, could give a full or shining account about the investment of these transfers by the recipient bank.

51. Turkish Lira

I CAME TO KNOW about the Turkish lira well before I left Geneva for Istanbul. Several well-meaning friends advised me, quite forcefully, that I should purchase while I was at Geneva all the Turkish lira I would need for my stay in Turkey. It was further advised that I should purchase some now, some later, some through others, but that I should always purchase Turkish lira in Geneva. This was my first acquaintance with the Turkish lira, though I refused to purchase even a single one in Geneva. The Turkish lira continued to fluctuate, sometimes mildly, sometimes wildly, sometimes even out of bounds, depending upon where you bought and sold it and what you did with what you got. This fluctuation was not good for the Turkish lira, but there it was. It was good, though, for those who planned for their good in this way.

The other thing I learned about the Turkish lira was never to say merely "lira." If you said lira as, for instance, in England you would say the pound, in the United States the dollar, in Switzerland the franc, and so on, you would immediately find that the listener would, in response, say Turkish lira. He would never correct you except in this general way. You said lira and he said Turkish lira. A few more mistakes and then you learned to say Turkish lira. You were never to be in any doubt that what you were talking about was the Turkish lira and not just the lira, and that you dare not separate the nation from its lira.

The Turkish lira is also called the Turkish pound, and if you ask which is correct, the reply would be that both are correct.

And if you persist, the further reply would be that Turkish lira when translated means Turkish pound. The Turkish lira has been devalued several times and there is constant talk of past, present, current, and expected devaluations. In the matter of devaluation, the nearest competitor of Turkey has been Israel.

52. The Customs

BEFORE I LEFT GENEVA for Istanbul, good friends advised me to take my car along and not to try to import it, I would have untold difficulties in getting what is known as *takrir* in Turkey (an official authorization or confirmation) so that the car could be imported duty free, a privilege to which I was entitled as a U.N. diplomat. I took this advice and drove into Istanbul on tourist plates, which later I had no difficulty in getting changed into regular diplomatic plates. While at Istanbul, I had no difficulty at any time in getting any *takrir* I wanted within a reasonable time. But in fairness to those who had difficulties, I must narrate some of the tales I heard and mention three or four instances of the Customs bureaucracy which I observed.

This is how one of the stories went (a true story, I was told). A car was imported for official use but the *takrir* could not be obtained for several months, nay some years, as a certain basic document had to receive the signature of every member of the cabinet. When most ministers had signed and there were just a few left, the government changed, and the whole process had to begin again.

A colleague of mine brought a car, driving in on some other type of plates which he used to call "ZZ plates." Every time he went out of Istanbul, he had to deposit the car at Customs and recover it on return. On one such return, I was with him when he went to drive away his car, having cleared all the necessary recovery procedure. But one of the tires was flat, so he went to seek a pump. To my surprise, he did not go in search of a garage but went directly to the same official with whom he had cleared the recovery papers. Without a word having been spoken by either of them, the official concerned brought out a pump from his table drawer. The tire was inflated and the pump returned with a note of ten Turkish lira. They both knew what had happened and what was expected of each other.

On one occasion I went along with a colleague to the airport Customs to pick up some bags that had arrived for me from Geneva. I was asked to identify the bags. The warehouse had hundreds of bags, but the intervention of my colleague melted the heart of a standing loader, who in consultation with the official concerned brought out the bags, which were lying behind their feet. Some Turkish lira had to be paid to the bookkeeping section of the department, and my colleague and I went to make the payment. But the books had been closed for the day and so we went the second day. When the payment had been made the books had to have seventeen signatures at different places and different junctions. The movement of the books to four different officials was involved.

A friend had been asked by a friend while still in the U.S.A. to clear the medical books which he had sent by ship. The friend at Istanbul found out that the clearing of the books would cost about 10,000 Turkish lira. The friend in the U.S.A. was astounded. So he wrote to the friend at Istanbul to await his arrival. When he arrived he went straight to the Customs and met the official concerned. No Turkish lira were mentioned but the dialogue went somewhat on the following lines:

"Which are the boxes you want to clear?"

After these were found (several days later):

"What do they contain?"

"Books."

"What books?"

"Medical books."

"Open them. What are these books?"

"Medical books."

"A list is required."

Some days later the owner of the medical books went back with a list.

"Is it typed?"

"No."

"A typed list is required."

Again, some days later another visit was made with the typed list.

"What does the list contain?"

"Titles of books." No.

"But what do the books contain? Lists of contents is required."

This too was prepared. But the new typed list did not contain the translation in Turkish. This was asked for and in due course provided. These are just the titles of sections, what of chapters, what of summary of the text? One must comply with the Turkish law with respect and in full.

Then the light dawned. What does the Turkish law say? It says that no proscribed or pornographic material should be permitted to enter Turkey. Hence, it is necessary to compare the list with the list of proscribed books. But insofar as pornographic material is concerned, how could its entry be prevented unless at least a summary was examined and such examination, therefore, required a summary in the Turkish language. When the law had been explained in such detail, the further explanations went on like this. Since the medical student did not have either the patience or the time or the skill to make such a translation of each of the three or four hundred books concerned, the best thing for him to do would be to authorize someone on his behalf to read selected passages, particularly those where illustrations of female form and organs appeared. The point of law would then perhaps be met.

On previous occasions it had been learned that such readers charged over 1,000 Turkish lira for every one hundred books but in this case if the importer were to pursue the matter further on his own, names of some selected readers could be given to him. It was cheaper to bear the burden of Turkish lira to ensure that no proscribed or pornographic material entered Turkey, reader or no reader.

On one occasion someone sent me a packet of incense sticks. As the worth was about ten Swiss francs, I did not think it worthwhile to get a *takrir*. Accompanied by a colleague I went to the officer concerned to take delivery, if necessary by paying the small duty that might be charged. But the matter was not one of duty. It was the Turkish law—either a *takrir* must be obtained or the regular procedure would be followed, which meant that the incense sticks would be sent to the official laboratory to determine their chemical content; then once the ingredients were known the duty would be charged according to the duty schedule applicable to each such ingredient. The simplest thing to do was to waive the whole matter, so I suggested that I was no longer interested and the incense sticks could be destroyed. But this was not acceptable to the administrator of the Turkish law. The item could not be destroyed; the analysis procedure was obligatory. In the end, I went and got a *takrir*.

53. Intermediaries

IT IS CUSTOMARY to go through intermediaries in Turkey. Who is the best for what is, of course, a matter of knowledge, selection, and good luck. Here are two episodes to which I was a witness.

A Bulgarian neighbor was the Consul of Bulgaria and his job

was to grant visas. His office was a few steps away from where we lived, so I had to pass by his office every day. There were always crowds, naturally, outside his office, and when I had to go in for my visa I saw for myself what a circuit it was. The intermediaries had taken over the outside so that one could benefit from the inside: to arrange the queue, to fill out the papers, to get them processed, to arrange *kebab* while one waited, to do all that was necessary to get you your visa.

The second episode was a more difficult one, though it was equally well accomplished through the good offices of an intermediary. A friend had to settle his income-tax matter. So he had found an intermediary (ideally a relative, and equally ideally one who had himself been an income-tax consultant or perhaps formerly even an official of the same office) and we met him outside the income-tax office. He led us to the counter of the official concerned. Two brief questions were asked and answered briefly. The papers were stamped and we left as quickly as we had mounted up the steps. It had all been beautifully fixed and, of course, the more brief the question and still briefer the answer, the larger must have been the intervention made by the intermediary and value for value paid.

Depending upon your needs and desires, fears and expectations, and likes and dislikes, as well as your patience threshold, find one excellent intermediary. He will find his own network of intermediaries to meet all your commands. Or else, find more than one for each of your situations or one for the fulfillment of every objective which you hold very high. But never do on your own what he or she can do for you. After all, an intermediary is an institution that has stood the test of time, and his importance must be respected.

54. Martial Law

MARTIAL LAW WAS IN EFFECT in Istanbul practically all the time I was there. For the pedestrian it meant he could cross the street. For the driver there was a little more order and a little more law on the road. The common man was unaware. The students were actively concerned with its continuance, as were the political leaders. The lawbreaker had to beware. The press had to observe.

The word *anarchy* began to be mentioned more and more. Now, anarchy has a great significance in Turkey for reasons which I did not fully understand, but the fact is that everyone seemed to understand and recognize anarchy when they saw it and some even when they did not see it.

I had a personal involvement with the martial law authority. One morning when I went to the office I was told that a member of the staff had not come because in the middle of the night the authorities had been to her apartment and taken her away. The question was whether anything should be done about it. I decided to go and see the Supreme Martial Law Authority of Istanbul. An appointment was made for the afternoon. He received me promptly in his personal office, accompanied by an aide.

I explained in English who I was, though he knew it already (it was mentioned to him when the appointment was made). Then came the crucial moment. I had already decided to make no request and raise no question, as the person concerned was a national of Turkey and she was not on the International Staff of the office. And yet, surely I had not gone to see him for nothing. I hoped that he would see my unspoken point. So I said (and here I reproduce words which I used, words which have remained in my mind as a part of my permanent memory bank) that this morning when I went to my office I was told, and here I took the name of the person concerned and simply stopped in the middle of the sentence. I had spoken in English, though his welcome had been in Turkish and he had given me no reason to believe that he knew English.

Having said this I got up. We shook hands formally and I left. I had decided that to say a word more to a man of honor, head of the martial law in Istanbul, a Turk, with complete powers, would have been both vain and in vain. When I returned to my office I told a colleague in private that my guess was that the lady would be back in her apartment in the earlier part of the night. This proved to be true. She was released and escorted back. The martial law had understood the request and had accepted it. No explanation was offered to the lady on her release, as none had been given to her on her arrest.

From the next day the martial law also placed a protection officer, fully armed, to protect me and my family. The officer stayed his shift, followed by another officer for the second shift, and the shifts went on for twenty-four hours for the next twelve months or more.

But then, some months later, the lady was again arrested by the martial law authorities and taken to jail, where she remained for several months. Finally she was put on trial and in due course was acquitted, released, and left alone to walk the path of her life more carefully in the future.

Several months later the same colleague was making a trip abroad. At the point of departure at the airport in Istanbul she was held back and not allowed to leave the country. She returned home and began reinforced efforts to establish her innocence again, and the following day, through the intervention of kind friends, she was let out, this time not out of prison, but out of Turkey.

55. Industrialization

IN ORDER TO KNOW THE FUTURE, you should look at the present and examine how much the past has been different from the present. If you looked inside Istanbul and went about thirty kilometers toward Bursa and spent a day at Bursa, or on the Asian side, you would see enough to appreciate the industrial scene. There are new modern enterprises, with young management and skilled personnel, enterprises based on technical collaboration with the West, technology as recent as the last decade or so, medium enterprises, small enterprises, interdependent enterprises, and enterprises ready to serve the consumer and the service needs of Turkey. These are all young enterprises and now almost out of the teething stage. Some are even exporting.

These enterprises are representative of what Turkey needs and what Turkey can do, in due course, with her own resources and on her own initiative. In a short time and within a short distance you would have seen the most representative and the most modern part of Turkey's industry, a complex that would, within its limitations of time and resources, do credit anywhere. You would also see the Fiats and the Renaults all assembled at Bursa—the Detroit of Turkey—with the aid of Italy in one case, and with the collaboration of France in the other. What you would have seen would seem quite clearly indicative of the successes ahead and the limitations yet to be overcome. You would have also seen that all of these enterprises are run by the Turks and for the Turks, something that future collaborators ought to remember well in spite of the Turkish fancy for that which is foreign.

However, it seemed that the initial development of new industry and the expansion of the existing industry had come almost to a dead halt as the years of my stay in Turkey progressed. It further seemed that outside capital was not moving in. The internal forces had not developed enough to take over. Some thought that the outsiders had done enough for Turkey and now it was up to the Turks. Some even thought that Turkey had not been appreciative enough of what others had done for it. Anyway, quite some internal revitalization would first need to be achieved before others would move in once more, since Turkey was no longer the first or the almost first choice of those who wanted to industrialize, at a quick profit, countries such as Turkey. The preferences had altered.

With so much water in and around, one would have expected Turkey to be a leading shipbuilder, but that was not the case. This would only further strengthen the view that Turkey's interest had been and continues to be greater in others' ships than in having ships of its own. It is also a fact that the conquests of Turkey even in the past owed more to its land forces than its naval fleets. The rest follows.

56. Strikes and Lockouts

THERE WERE NO MAJOR STRIKES, and even the small ones did not take place during the time martial law was imposed, as the authorities did not wish to see any interference with law and order. But when martial law was relaxed or absent, two or three worthwhile strikes did take place—in the auto industry, for instance—which showed that the words, sentiments, and thoughts that I had heard in several meetings were capable of fulfillment. Normally, given freedom of action (even when not so openly given), industrial action would be taken in Istanbul and in other parts of Turkey because the reason for it existed and would continue to exist. As regards lockouts, these being an outmoded form of employer action, a dead inheritance of word and thought from the past, there was no room for them with or without the martial law.

57. Holding Companies

IN THE FIRST FLUSH of industrialization, expansion, and commercialization, the holding companies, operating from Istanbul, played a significant role, though it was said that whatever was worth holding was held by a single holding company. But lately this situation too has been changing, and the existing ones were doing no more than what they did before nor were any new ones emerging on any worthwhile scale. Capital investment had become scarce.

But you must not conclude that the banks did not have enough money to lend. They had more than most on their hands but there were no big borrowers. And without big borrowers there could not be any new industrialization, expansion, and commercialization. The government was trying to do what the holding companies and big business had been doing before, but the types were different, the levels of operation were not the same, and different things had to be done irrespective of comparative costs.

58. Migrant Workers

THE TURK IS NOT MIGRATORY, by nature or by habit. And so when the Turkish workers went abroad it was not clear why they were called the migrant workers. The Turk does not move; he is completely stable. If he moves, he comes back. Until he comes back, or in the extreme when he does not or cannot come back, he always takes with him part of Turkey and Turks from Turkey. In this case perhaps it was indicative of the wish and the hope that the Turkish workers would settle down abroad and Turkey would colonize other countries, especially West Germany, for whom they have an affinity and admiration. For these and other reasons to back up the hope, the governmental and trade union leaders went overseas from time to time to see the Turkish workers in their new homes, urging them to do better and to settle down and to get more Turkish workers and to have the best of Turkey with them. That is why efforts were made to improve their status in West Germany and to better their conditions of living, to improve their wages and social security benefits, and even to help them to have their own Turkish way of living. A newspaper in Turkish also put in its appearance, printed on foreign soil.

But they came to be called guest workers. The Turkish workers abroad, in spite of their numbers and length of stay and the support they provided to the employer, became the guest workers in the host country.

It was believed that many more than 700,000 Turkish workers had gone to work abroad, mostly in West Germany. Some went once, others twice, and others more. Some stayed for short terms, others for some years. Turkish workers went with their skills, but quite some large numbers of unskilled workers were also a part of those who went abroad. They went by the hundreds, sometimes by the thousands. They went in special Turkish Airlines flights from special departure halls, and when they returned on holiday or forever, there were special arrival halls for them too. They were so many.

They went to find arranged employment; assured Turkish community life, good wages, cheap housing and cheap living, they went in high spirits, happy and well. They earned well. They saved well. They came on holidays to Turkey but back they went again, as often as they could. It was wonderful that so many could go. And they could bring back home (send too) so much foreign exchange.

On their return, they brought back Mercedes cars, furniture, clothes, electronics, tools and toys and chocolates. Their women and children were happy, their parents and neighbors delighted with the achievement of their own kith and kin. The government was happy that with this foreign exchange their external currency requirements were being met. The employment situation in Turkey was not causing any hardship. The Turkish lira was able to look the American dollar in the face and even stand up to it. The withdrawal of the American forces and the pressure of the United States was of no consequence, therefore. Wealth was going into villages. Prosperity was spreading.

It was as it should be. The banks were happy that they were having good business when the foreign exchange began to flow into the country. The traffic acquired a glamor too, with such a large number of Mercedes on the city roads. New links had been formed and old ones strengthened, and Germany would always be appreciative of what Turkey had done for them. Government representatives and trade union leaders from West Germany began to make reciprocal visits. The West German system even made arrangements for the Turkish workers to become better informed while still in Germany just before they returned, and on return were willing to lend assistance to those who had served them so well. Everyone could go. There was no end to demand. And there was universal acclaim and recognition for Turkey and the Turkish workers.

It was a state of total euphoria. When the five hundred thousandth (or some other equally impressive number) worker was going to West Germany, a ceremonial sendoff was arranged at the Istanbul Airport, at which I had the honor to be present together with the then Minister of Labor, who had specially come over to join the ceremony, with TV, radio, and photo coverage, and garlands and good wishes.

But alas, it did not last, as no euphoria does. In this case it could not, nor was it expected to. It was visible from a long distance and quite far ahead that the flood would become a flow and the flow a trickle and the trickle come a dead stop. But no one was prepared to prepare for it. The going was so good, so hypnotizing. There was profit, so much profit that no one planned to turn it into assets. When it was on, for whatever else it did, it did not create new industrialization in Turkey or any expansion of what was there before. Employment opportunities declined (some thought that about 20 percent of the labor force was jobless and that the percentage would increase) and inflation grew.

While in Germany the workers did not become graduates or diploma holders. They did not become specialists. Their skills did not go beyond what they began with. Languages were not learned. Blueprints for times ahead were not prepared. On return, new small-scale enterprises were not opened, nor new technology introduced in handicrafts. Standards of performance remained as they were, hopes continued to remain hopes.

But with their return, the pressure on the domestic employment market grew; also pressure on housing, the social security system, demand for imported goods, foreign cigarettes, *raki* and wine and whisky, and petrol for Mercedes cars and other luxuries. The demand for marriages, the greatest luxury of all, also grew by leaps and bounds. The apartments were sold at desired prices. The streets were full of people.

But in this way equilibrium was restored. That which belonged to villages was theirs. The city of Istanbul got back the skills it had lost. The Turkish economy had profited. The banks had opened more branches. It was time to live again and live well, for the time when West Germany would call them once more.

59. Computers

COMPUTERS ARE A SIGN OF MODERNIZATION, high standards, expectations for the future, intensive utilization of resources, industrialization, Americanization, Westernization, and Europeanization, as well as many other things. These are also a sign of status and prestige and being one with the best. In Istanbul, and of course in Ankara, there are many computers, installed and used for one or more or all of the reasons mentioned above. These reflect well on the makers and their sellers and the promoters of computers. They also reflect well on the farsighted ones who have them and who make use of them.

But the underutilization of computers is significant, maybe no more significant than in several other cities and countries, but it should be a matter of concern and cost to those who buy and those who sell and those who bear the cost of computers. The more this concern is taken seriously, the more will computers be used and the more will they serve the objectives of modernization.

60. Seminars

THE TURKS LIKE DISCUSSIONS, meetings, conferences, congresses, conventions, and seminars. So I went along with them. I was with Turks most of the time both at Istanbul and Ankara, in discussions covering the largest possible variety of subjects and in meetings and conferences and conventions organized by them. I observed and listened and learned.

I also organized several seminars with them; some with trade unions, others with employer organizations, still others with government representatives, some even with all concerned with the subject of the seminars—horizontal ones, vertical ones, and ones that went beyond the national level and even ones on themes of limited interest.

The participation was complete and frank, the discussions far-reaching, the spirit one of cooperation and understanding. But one could not force conclusions or plans of action or follow-up. One had to wait for inner realization, sequences that time will reveal, and let events overpower and overtake. It was don't rush the pace, don't even mark it out step by step.

Seminars, meetings, conferences, congresses, conventions, and discussions bring people together, create awareness and awakening. These are rewards enough.

61. State Monopolies

ELSEWHERE IF YOU ARE A MONOPOLY, you would like to hide this fact, and when the fact gets around you would like to have it suppressed. If you do not in some countries, the state will be after you. In any case, even the most recognized and well-established monopolies do not like to be called monopolies. When the state has a monopoly it is called a public utility, a public service, a public institution, but never a state monopoly. In Turkey, however, a state monopoly is called a state monopoly. The state monopolies in Turkey sell at state monopoly shops—liquor, wine, cigarettes, cigars, and tea—all items that have an excise duty on them. These items and similar items are sold also at other shops, though the brands may vary. Recently, the state monopolies have set up duty-free shops at airports and shops for diplomats.

When you see a long line, growing longer each day, beginning in the morning and ending at closing hours, and the line is an orderly one, you will recognize that it is the line for the state monopolies. In Istanbul, this line is at the most prominent, central, and famous place—that is, at Taksim. You will notice if you are a keen observer that from day to day the same persons line up in large numbers. Some even come three or four times each day. They are the persons who come for cigarettes. On each occasion they get two packs; thus, in a day they collect six or eight packs. This is their daily wage, their total earnings.

These cigarette packs then find their ways to counter sale, open sale, sale by sitting and standing vendors at key places. Big shops, cinema centers, post offices, open spaces, *dolmus* stations, newspaper stands, bus stops have regulars standing and selling cigarette packs which they got at the state monopolies.

This process of lining up will go on without interruption, and the state monopolies will sell so many cartons each day. If more were sold, the daily price at the stands would fall. This has become a system now. The cigarettes are in great demand but short supply. The price is regulated. The state monopolies alone sell them (the brand they deal in). People want this particular brand; and there are people who wish to make their living this way. Above all, people have money to pay for what they desire. No one is hurt. No tempers are lost. No police intervention takes place. The lines are orderly and take place in a prominent area. They even lend color and image to the product and to the state monopolies.

62. Turkish Poppies

HAVING GIVEN UP the American Project for the Prevention of Cultivation of Turkish Poppies, the Turkish government now allows, on a regulated basis, the cultivation of Turkish poppies for the use of the drug industry in Turkey and elsewhere.

Turkish poppies are lovely to look at. The farmers are proud of their cash crop, which benefits them substantially and raises them in the respect of others. They would like the demand to rise as fast as possible and go as far as it possibly can. They would like to be the monopoly producers. It would bring fame and credit to them and their country. They would be the best regular supplier of the United States and European countries. The part they play in meeting the demands of the affluent ones is very important indeed.

The poppy when young and green has soft, tender miniseeds, pretty white granules. These, when eaten tender, are a delight of the young and the old. When pounded and mixed with milk and sugar and turned into a sweet, it is a real treat for all. It brings good health and peace of mind. It is a welcome luxury in all homes that can afford it and know how to benefit from it.

When in other hands, there are bitter consequences for those who eat the poppy fruit: the men and women, teenagers and youth who become addicted to what they take. This makes them drug addicts—of danger to themselves, of grief to their families, and of great consequence to society. All because they took the products made from poppies.

63. Frontiers

IN ORDER TO UNDERSTAND Turkey, it is essential to know the character of the people of Turkey and the frontiers of Turkey, as frontiers have a great influence on the whole situation.

To understand this subject well, it is best to take a good look at as many frontiers as possible (general and particular), land and sea (and the bridges to cross over the water and over land too), frontiers with other countries, frontiers within the country, extended frontiers, frontiers by courtesy, frontiers of religion, economic frontiers, frontiers made by minorities, empire frontiers, and even the new frontiers. It is also good to go back a little in history and thus, perhaps, be able to look ahead at emerging frontiers as well.

Frontiers and some landmarks of the past have been identified by names in a process of selective mention of names, incidents, and episodes because of their mark on Turkey and on the people of Turkey and their significance in the Turkey of today and their importance in the understanding of the Turkish way of life.

Turkey is the only country in the world which is called, by those who should know, the Republic of Europe and Asia. It is the only Asian country with an encroachment on Europe. In addition, Turkey is a democracy. Turkey is also called the Republic of the Middle East. After the completion of the Bridge of Bosphorus, Turkey is now truly the bridge between Europe and Asia.

Turkey is in the southwest of Asia and the southeast of Europe. Iraq is to the southeast; Syria is to the south. Greece and Bulgaria are in the northwest; the U.S.S.R. is in the northeast. Iran is also to the east. The Aegean Sea is in the west. The Black Sea is in the north. The Mediterranean Sea is in the south. Lest it be forgotten, there is one more sea with which Turkey is concerned, the Sea of

Marmara. This sea is not a frontier of Turkey but lies within its frontiers. Its significance, however, is as great as that of any frontier. Through it you can go to the Black Sea, passing through the Bosphorus. You can also go to the Aegean Sea and the Mediterranean Sea through it if you are prepared to let the Strait of Dardanelles be your guide.

The entry for the U.S.S.R., Rumania, and Bulgaria to the Black Sea and the Sea of Marmara from the Mediterranean Sea and the Aegean Sea lies through the Bosphorus. Equally important is the fact that the entry from the Black Sea and the Sea of Marmara for the Aegean Sea and the Mediterranean Sea is vital for the U.S.S.R., essential for Rumania, and important for Bulgaria.

The Bosphorus, the Golden Horn, the Sea of Marmara, and the Dardanelles Strait, all captive waters of Turkey, separate Europe from Asia. Together these form a continuous uninterrupted water link between the Black Sea and the Mediterranean Sea and are waterways of the greatest significance.

Northeastern Turkey includes part of Armenia. Southeastern Asian Turkey includes parts of Kurdistan. Moreover, there is the European Turkey and the Asian Turkey. Asian Turkey consists of 97 percent of Turkey; only 3 percent of Turkey is European Turkey. Modern Turkey, long known as Asia Minor, has only a tiny trace in Europe and the rest is all in Asia. Only that part of Istanbul corresponding to historic Constantinople is situated entirely on the European side. The center of West Asian Turkey includes Anatolia, which is one of the oldest inhabited regions of the world. And the southeast of Turkey is drained by the upper courses of the Tigris and Euphrates rivers, which touch other countries and other shores.

It was at the Treaty of Sèvres in 1920, between the Ottoman Empire on the one hand and the Allies (excluding Russia and America) on the other, that the Ottoman Empire was liquidated and Turkish sovereignty abolished over many countries and many lands. Among other matters, Turkey was to grant autonomy to Kurdistan, and Armenia became a separate republic under international guarantees. Turkey renounced sovereignty over Mesopotamia (Iraq) and Palestine (including Trans-Jordan), which became British protectorates, and over Syria (including Lebanon), which became a French mandate. Turkey ceded certain parts to Greece and certain other parts to Italy. Of course, the treaty was rejected by the nationalist government of Kemal Ataturk, who, as President of the Republic from 1923 until his death in 1938, was responsible for many reforms and the modernization of Turkey. This rejection and the separate treaty with the U.S.S.R. and the subsequent victories against the Greeks forced the Allies to negotiate a new treaty in 1923, the Treaty of Lausanne in Switzerland.

Finally, Cyprus, while neither a frontier on land or on sea, is not far away and in some ways is already close enough to cause hopes and desires (apart from conflict) in many hearts. How much would Turkey like Cyprus also to become its frontier, an inner one best of all!

Turkey separates Europe from Asia and stands in between the two, with its 97 percent Asian and 3 percent European territory. But it does much more too: Islam and Christianity and Judaism and other shades of religion meet in Turkey. While Turkey stands between the East and the West, the East and the West also meet in Turkey. The old and the new of Turkey and her neighbors of past and present shake each other's hands in Turkey. If the communist world is in the north, the Arab world is not far either —it stands on the south.

Every border confers some benefit. When there are more than one, sometimes they cancel each other out. It is important who is across the border. When you have many borders you have many strengths and many weaknesses. In the case of Turkey, fortunately for all concerned, the strengths outweigh the weaknesses.

Bosphorus

The Bosphorus Strait is one of the most important straits in the world; as a passage point it is extremely important. Incidentally, the only other strait in this part of the world is also in Turkey, that is the Dardanelles Strait. On both sides of the Bosphorus and its entrance into the Sea of Marmara stands Istanbul. It is the Bosphorus of Istanbul that leads you into the Black Sea. In addition to the many important things the Bosphorus does, it divides Istanbul and, as some would say more forcefully than others, the Bosphorus divides Turkey too, into two separate or even two continuing parts.

The Bosphorus is the destiny of Istanbul, and of Turkey. The Bosphorus is Istanbul, all the way through, and Istanbul is Turkey, and a great deal of Turkey lies within the heart of Istanbul. So I made its acquaintance in a comprehensive way to realize first-hand and in some detail its importance, its length, its breadth and depth, its impact on Turkish life and attitudes. On the European side I walked in patches, all the way through, from end to end, some parts many times over, spending many afternoons and evenings, having lunches, sometimes dinner, on the Bosphorus. I drove through in my car, by bus, by *dolmus*, by taxi, and did the boat trips from the beginning of Bosphorus to its end on the European side. Across I went by boat and by ship, and by car when the Bosphorus Bridge was completed. While on the Asian side, I drove from end to end, visiting landmarks, important sites, junctions, points of interest, and centers of military strategy. It was not possible to see the Bosphorus enter the Black Sea from the Asian side unless one was able to do so from military stations, and this was not possible.

Now about some physical properties of the Bosphorus. It is 29.9 kilometers long. It is only 640 meters wide at the narrowest point. It is deep enough (with a swift current and a very deep central channel) for most things to pass through but not deep enough for too many secret movements, at least for those who are not Turks. As it gets ready to meet the Black Sea, it narrows down somewhat. On the other side it merges into the Sea of Marmara. Where it narrows most it becomes the Golden Horn.

The Bosphorus has a protocol for those who wish to use it, and there is strict control over who should enter when and who should go out next. Through the Bosphorus pass ships carrying cargo, arms, and airplanes. Submarines come and go through the Bosphorus. Ships of the navy use it frequently. Holiday makers too use the Bosphorus for pleasure. The Bosphorus is watched, naturally, by an Overlord, during both day and night and from both sides.

The watch continues even when you leave the Bosphorus, more on the side of the Sea of Marmara where it extends to the Dardanelles and a little on the Aegean Sea too. In the case of the Black Sea you can go without the Overlord seeing all he may want to see unless you are close to the Turkish side, but that is your own affair. The Overlord knows who is going (and from where he is coming), what he is carrying (to a certain extent but not the whole of it), whether the interest of Turkey is greater or lesser in any such movement, how far he is going (how far he should be watched), and sometimes how far he has been (as only the friends of Turkey can go, the foes need not be mentioned).

Apart from Turkey, it is worthwhile to know who the users of the Bosphorus are. If the Americans (whether from the Aegean Sea or the Mediterranean Sea and the seas beyond) wish to go to the Black Sea, they must go through the Bosphorus. And having gone into the Black Sea, they cannot go into any other sea or waterway unless the Overlord lets them first return to the Bosphorus and then continue. The other great power, with even greater dependence on the Bosphorus, is the U.S.S.R. The U.S.S.R. simply cannot leave the Black Sea, whatever the contingency or purpose, except through the Bosphorus.

Both the U.S.A. and the U.S.S.R. need the services of the Bosphorus and the goodwill of Turkey. The Bosphorus is also needed by Rumania and Bulgaria and one might then draw a little on imagination to connect this need with the needs of some other Eastern Euroupeans countries. Hence, the Bosphorus is the destiny of Istanbul and of Turkey. In order to widen your understanding of the Bosphorus, you must imagine what would happen if it were incapacitated, taken over, inefficient, in undesirable hands, ignored, bypassed, unprotected; in short, if it were not in the capable hands of the Turks of Turkey. You must also know the extent of comprehensive service provided by Turkey through the Bosphorus: Overlord, Monitor, Census Authority, one who never lets you go out of mind, not even out of sight to any large extent, who has charted your path each way.

Should you wish to go from one part of Istanbul to another or from one part of Turkey to another, there is now the Bosphorus Bridge to cross. The Bosphorus with its new bridge has added to the greatness and the strength of Istanbul and Turkey by providing a roadway (in addition to the waterway) that leads the trucks and the trade from one part of Europe to that part of the East and Asia which has the Turkish roads leading into their country and merging with them. The Bosphorus Bridge is the only road communication available to Bulgaria and what lies behind Bulgaria, the whole of Eastern Europe and beyond. Trucks carry essentials even from the U.S.A., Canada, the U.N., France, Netherlands, Germany, Italy, Yugoslavia, and others who wish to send what could best be sent by road. Thousands of trucks carry essential commercial goods, military goods, and even goods on secret mission pass every month over the Bosphorus Bridge and through Istanbul. The return journey may not be vital, but the trucks must return to come again, and they bring goods from countries as far out as Afghanistan.

When the Bosphorus Bridge was opened, on a cold morning when hundreds of dignitaries led by the President of Turkey, those who had come from Turkey and from countries around Turkey and beyond, the weight of destiny was so great that the bridge began to sway (some even said swing) when each one passed over it. I found that I was walking along with others and in good company, with a joyous movement caused not by my own effort alone but by the weight of the walkers in their totality. The Bosphorus Bridge, one of the largest suspension bridges of the world (1,074 meters long) was opened in 1973 and is expected to carry, by 1995 (some say even by 1985 if the oil lasts), 34 million vehicles.

This evaluation and understanding of the Bosphorus should make it easier to understand and appreciate certain parts of the Turkish character and of his great country. Who else has such a gift of God! When you realize the extent of dependence of the two superpowers, great countries that they are, on Turkey's Bosphorus, you will also realize at least some of the important features of the Turkish character. Allah gave Istanbul the Bosphorus and put it where it would do most for all Turks and their neighbors. But the Turks have given themselves the bridge over the Bosphorus. Credit be to all givers.

Black Sea

The Black Sea is an inland sea covering practically the whole of the north of Turkey. The Black Sea has the U.S.S.R. on its north and Turkey on its south. It makes the important frontier between Turkey and the U.S.S.R. The Black Sea has great importance for the U.S.S.R. and for the U.S.A.

Insofar as Turkey is concerned, the Turks go on holiday boats to the Black Sea. They have other uses for the Black Sea too. But the Turks also do a lot for the Black Sea. Turkey provides the only sea passage from the Black Sea to the Mediterranean Sea.

Golden Horn

The Horn of Africa is turbulent. However, there is another Horn that is its opposite: the Golden Horn of Istanbul, called golden because in Turkey all that glitters is gold. But it is a true

Horn, too. It is here where, on one side, the Bosphorus tapers off to its terminus inland and merges with Istanbul.

The Golden Horn, its waters flowing under the Galata Bridge, goes quite some distance into the hinterland and is an inlet of the Bosphorus; it enables the Turkish way of life to flourish on its two sides, with its four-mile-long harbor to the north of the promontory on which Istanbul stands.

A sunset on the Golden Horn is a truly golden one.

Sea of Marmara

The Sea of Marmara is within the frontiers of Turkey. This inland sea, only 280 kilometers long and no more than 80 kilometers wide, separates Turkey in Europe from Turkey in Asia. On the one side, it leads Turkey to the Dardanelles, onto the Agean Sea, and beyond to the Mediterranean Sea. On the other side, it takes Turkey through the Bosphorus of Turkey right into the nearby Black Sea.

There are many who wish to be on friendly terms with the Sea of Marmara so that they, their ships, and the ships' cargoes can pass through safely and happily.

Dardanelles Strait

This strip of water has a strategic location for Turkey. It is 60 kilometers long and just 1.6 kilometers wide at its narrowest. With its shores formed by the Galipoli Peninsula on the northwest and the mainland of Turkey in Asia, it binds together the Sea of Marmara and the Aegean Sea. It is sometimes called the Turkish Strait, though some others prefer its other name, the Dardanelles Strait.

It was by the Treaty of Lausanne in 1923 that the Dardanelles zone was restored to Turkey on the understanding that it would remain demilitarized. Secretly, however, Turkey soon began to fortify the zone, and in 1936, by the Montreux Convention,

Turkey was formally permitted to remilitarize it. Incidentally, since 1402 the Dardanelles, with brief interruptions, has remained under Turkish hands.

Aegean Sea

The Aegean Sea, which is regarded as an arm of the Mediterranean Sea, is between Greece and Turkey and separates the two countries-in-conflict. The Aegean Sea is connected to the Dardanelles Strait (Turkish waters) and through the Dardanelles the connection goes deeper on account of the link with the Sea of Marmara, the inland sea of Turkey. And of course for those who must use this sea route to go to the Mediterranean Sea from the Black Sea, this is the only sea passage.

Mediterranean Sea

The Mediterranean Sea is regarded as an inland sea—the world's largest—but because of its many connections and outlets it gives access to almost everyone, anywhere in the world. And through one of its important connections, passing through the Aegean Sea (which, in turn, is regarded as one of its chief divisions), the Dardanelles Strait, the Sea of Marmara, and the Bosphorus (the route followed by many), it links with the Black Sea. That is how the inland Mediterranean Sea has wide accesses. Turkey happens to be minding its own business well on strategic rules such as these.

Russia

Because of the small part of Turkey which is Europe, it can be said that in the whole Western (European) Alliance and in the whole European Economic Community (EEC), Turkey is the only country that has a border and a frontier, and a long one too, with the U.S.S.R. The northern frontier of Turkey is the southern frontier of the U.S.S.R. The U.S.S.R. has a great interest in the Black Sea, in the Bosphorus of Turkey, the Golden Horn of

Istanbul, the Sea of Marmara, and the Dardanelles Strait. Turkey has certain neighbors who are of permanent interest to the U.S.S.R. Quite a few citizens of the U.S.S.R. speak Turkish. Two republics of the U.S.S.R., Armenia and Georgia, have common land borders with Turkey at the north. And that which concerns these two southern republics is the concern of the whole of Russia.

Who has not heard of the Russo-Turkish Wars and the attempts that were made by Russia to find an outlet on the Black Sea and, in later stages, to gain control of the Dardanelles and the Bosphorus straits? Conflicts and wars continued from the seventeenth century. It was only in 1921 that the U.S.S.R., as the result of the Treaty of Friendship with Turkey, returned certain districts to Kemal Ataturk's Turkish government.

The relations with the U.S.S.R. continued to be cordial until World War II. But after Turkey declared war on Germany and Japan in February 1945, and March 1945 when the U.S.S.R. denounced its earlier Friendship Treaty of 1921 and demanded a thorough revision of the Montreux Convention and joint control of the Straits, the relations between Turkey and the U.S.S.R. became acrimonious. Events moved swiftly in Turkey in the next few years and then, in 1952, Turkey became a full member of the North Atlantic Treaty Organization (NATO). It is only recently, in 1974, that while maintaining close relations with the U.S.A., efforts were made by the Turks at the same time to cultivate better relations with the U.S.S.R.

Iran

Iran is a neighbor of Turkey, and they have common neighbors too in the U.S.S.R. and Iraq. Like Turkey, Iran was a member of the Central Treaty Organization (CENTO) while it lasted. Iran is the second-largest country in the Middle East.

From 1037–55, Iran (then Persia) came under the Seljuk Turks. The Empire was, however, broken up in the twelfth century. Armenia in the sixteenth century was divided between Persians

(Iranians) and Turks, Russia owning a portion during the nineteenth century. Iran and Turkey have thus had a common history at least a part of the way.

Islam is the official religion of Iran, and though that is not the case in Turkey, Islam binds the people of Turkey to the people of Iran. If 99 percent of the people of Turkey are Muslims, the Muslims in Iran are no less than 98 percent of the population.

Iran imports goods which pass through Turkey. The carpets of Turkey and the carpets of Iran are world famous. While Turkey concentrates on wool, Iran has taken to silk, though both of them continue to hold world markets because female labor is cheap in the carpet industry in the two countries.

Major earthquakes have unfortunately shaken both Iran and Turkey from time to time. Thus, there are common underground frontiers between the two countries which have common elements leading to malfunctioning of the earth under these two neighbors.

Iran has 2 million Kurds as against the 4 million in Turkey, the 2 million in Iraq, and another 250,000 in Syria. Whereas in Iran the Armenians are a sect, there are about 70,000 Armenians in Turkey, 130,000 in Syria, and in the U.S.S.R. there is the whole Armenian Soviet Socialist Republic. It is also estimated that about 100,000 Armenians have already emigrated to the U.S.A.

These are matters not only of common interest but of great importance in the times ahead.

Iraq

Turkey is to the north of Iraq, and in the uplands of the northeast is Iraqi Kurdistan. Both Iraq and Turkey have Kurds as a part of their population. While there are 4 million Kurds in Turkey, there are no less than 2 million in Iraq. Most of the population of Iraq is Muslim. The Turks form one of the large minorities of Iraq, and many people of Iraq speak Turkish.

In the nineteenth century the Turkish administration came to be enforced in three provinces of Iraq—Basra, Baghdad, and Mosul. Iraq is thus a former Turkish province. In World War I the British invaded Iraq in their war against the Ottoman Empire. In 1920, the Treaty of Sèvres established Iraq as a mandate of the League of Nations under British administration. In 1955, Turkey and Iraq formed the Baghdad Pact. This treaty was joined by Iran, Pakistan, and Britain. Although Iraq left the Baghdad Pact in 1959, Turkey and Iraq continue as good friends. After Iraq left, the remaining allies renamed themselves as CENTO.

The Baghdad Railway begins at Istanbul and ends at Baghdad. Iraq has a land route to Europe through Turkey's Bosphorus Bridge, and when Europe wishes to ensure flow of goods to Iraq, the trucks must go via Turkey. Iraq is a country rich in oil, and the resources of oil are welcome when they lie within reach in a neighbor's courtyard.

Syria

From the fifteenth to the thirteenth centuries B.C. Syria was probably a part of the Empire of the Hittites. By the late eleventh century, the Seljuk Turks had captured most of Syria. In 1516 the Ottoman Empire annexed the area, which continued to belong to the Turks until 1918. During World War I, the British encouraged the Syrian nationalists to fight against the Ottoman Empire. In 1920, France received a League of Nations mandate over the Levant States (roughly, present-day Syria and Lebanon). The Sanjak of Alexandretta came to Turkey in 1939.

Seventy-five percent of Syrians are Muslim Arabs (the Christians are 15 percent), that is, their religion is Islam. Syria has about 250,000 Kurds as against 4 million in Turkey. While Turkey has only about 70,000 Armenians, in Syria the number is 130,000. As is well known, the Kurds and the Armenians are important even when they are in a minority.

Turkey is the land route for Syria to Europe, and, with the Bridge of Bosphorus, Syria can get what is needed in a hurry.

Syria is an important friendly neighbor, and the Syrian role in the affairs of the Middle East, in Lebanon, and in what goes on between the Israelis and the Arabs is of worldwide importance.

Bulgaria

Bulgaria is another neighbor of Turkey, and if the relations between Turkey and Bulgaria ever deteriorated, the Bosphorus Bridge would not have the opportunity to carry all that it does, on the way to Europe, for instance.

In 1014, Bulgaria was absorbed into the Byzantine Empire. Later, Bulgaria passed under Ottoman rule until the national revival of the nineteenth century resulted in the creation of an autonomous principality under Turkish suzerainty in 1878. Then in 1912–13, Bulgaria assisted in the defeat of the Turks. By the Treaty of Lausanne of 1923, about 800,000 Turks living in Bulgaria and Greece were resettled in Turkey, mostly unskilled peasants. About 200,000 persons in present-day Bulgaria speak Turkish.

Greece

Turkey and Greece have faced each other for a long time— sometimes winning, sometimes losing. The dispute in the Aegean Sea over the exploration for oil was preceded by the Turks taking over 40 percent of Cyprus against the will and determination of the Greeks. So the Turks and the Greeks live in Cyprus, divided as before, the Turks better off now than the Greeks. While this has been going on, there are Greeks living in Istanbul as Greek-Turks, prospering from the economic situation there.

Istanbul and Greece are connected by land frontiers (and the traffic flows). Greece and Turkey favor some common cuisine, and 20,000 Greeks speak the Turkish language.

Going back some centuries, to 1453, the Turks captured Constantinople, and by 1460 they had conquered all Greece. Except for some few years Greece remained Turkish until the outbreak of the War of Independence in 1821. British, French, and Russian intervention in 1827 led to the establishment of Greek independence in 1829. The war of 1897 ended in disaster for Greece, but the Balkan Wars of 1912–13 won for Greece most of the disputed areas.

The Greeks, encouraged by the Allies, launched an offensive against Turkey. The counter-offensive, beginning in August 1922, ended with the complete rout of the Greeks. Then followed the negotiations at Lausanne. By the agreement reached in Lausanne in 1923, approximately 1.5 million Greeks living in Turkey were repatriated to Greece and approximately 800,000 Turks living in Greece and Bulgaria were resettled in Turkey.

Getting back to the present, both Turkey and Greece belong to NATO, and both Turkey and Greece are also associate members of the EEC. Greece and Turkey have common interests and ambitions. How to reconcile these, retaining advantages for each of them, is the problem.

Rumania

Bulgaria is a neighbor of Turkey and Rumania is a neighbor of Bulgaria. Like Bulgaria, Rumania depends on the use of the Black Sea. Also like Bulgaria, Rumania needs the roadways of Turkey for getting to Turkey's Middle East neighbors.

The Princes of Wallachia in 1417 and of Moldavia in the mid-sixteenth century became vassals of the Ottoman Empire. An ill-fated alliance in 1711 of these princes with Peter I of Russia led to Turkish domination of Rumania. And then events followed as times moved. Even today, some Rumanians speak Turkish and a few Turks speak Rumanian; there is even a small Turkish minority in Rumania.

64. Extended Frontiers

MENTION MUST BE MADE of certain other frontiers—political, military, and economic, frontiers of the past and the present. And certain other frontiers of courtesy also deserve to be mentioned —countries from which Turkey has borrowed something of importance, perhaps given something in return. A little word would be of advantage at least about some of the leaders of the countries of the European Economic Community, in view of Turkey's being an associate member. Something about the earlier times and the times of the empires, about minorities, brotherhoods, and alliances must also be mentioned as a part of the extended frontiers of Turkey.

Certain selected snatches and snippets have been put together in order to show what needs to be seen. By placing something together and something apart, by hopping, skipping, and scattering, patterns have been formed to highlight specific features of importance.

America

In 1917, the U.S.A. had nearly severed relations with Turkey, but the countries were not at war. After 1941, Turkey received lend-lease aid from the U.S.A. And despite considerable Allied pressure, Turkey declared war on Germany only in February 1945. In 1946 Turkey became the recipient of the U.S.A. assistance under the Truman Doctrine. Partly as the result of aid under the Marshall Plan (European Recovery Program), the Turkish economy expanded considerably after 1950. And by 1971 the U.S.A. had given Turkey about $5.7 billion in aid under various programs. In 1952 Turkey became a full member of the North Atlantic Treaty Organization. U.S. air and missile bases were subsequently established in Turkey.

If the U.S.A. has not been active in Turkey to the same extent as, for instance, England has been, the explanation lies in the late intervention of the U.S.A. in European and Middle Eastern affairs. But once the U.S.A. moved in, its influence in Turkey became quite substantial. Equally, the assistance given by the U.S.A. has also been significant. In Istanbul, there is the American Hospital and Roberts College as a mark of the active presence of the U.S.A. in Turkey. At Ankara, there is the Middle East (Technical) University, which has also received assistance from the U.S.A. In addition, the Haceteppe University at Ankara has been a large beneficiary of American help. The U.S.A. has, through its military activity, helped Ankara, Istanbul, and other places to prosper in several ways—infrastructure, production, services, facilities, training, confidence in performance, and the like.

As the result of U.S. pressure, the growing of opium poppies in Turkey was banned in 1971 (effective 1972), an act heavily subsidized by the U.S.A. In 1974, however, Turkey announced that it would allow cultivation of opium poppies under state control for medical purposes.

The U.S.A. is one of the important users of the waters of Turkey, the most important being the Bosphorus. America is also a leading trade partner of Turkey. The Turkish lira has already suffered a loss of value, and now the American dollar is also facing a serious decline in its purchasing power on the foreign markets.

France

French is still the language of Turkish diplomacy. In collaboration with France Renault cars are being produced in large numbers, close to Istanbul. The French Renaults built in Istanbul are popular with those who cannot afford the Mercedes (the only active competitor of the Renaults in Istanbul is the Italian Fiat, also built near Istanbul). The French Consulate is one of the largest in Istanbul and stands at the entrance to the Street of Freedom, with an eye on Taksim Square. There is a French hospital, children go to French schools, and adults take French courses. The writer Pierre Loti of France is well known in Istanbul for the legacy he has left to the city of his love. There was the "French Connection" and there has also been the "Poppy Connection."

Though times may have changed, it is still recalled in history that France used to be called the traditional ally of Turkey, but there is no need for that type of ally anymore. France, however, continues to be one of the supporters of Turkey in the EEC. (France is a leading member of the EEC, while Turkey is an associate member.)

Germany

At one time in the now distant past the reorganization of the Turkish army was in the hands of German officers. Germany had substantial influence in Ottoman affairs, and the Baghdad Railway was built by German interests. In 1926 Turkey adopted (largely unchanged) the German Code of Commercial Law. In February 1945, Turkey declared war on Germany.

Today, Germany is liked and even envied by the Turks. Germany employed the largest number of Turkish workers. Even though Turkey would have been happier if the Turkish workers had not been returned, Turkey does not carry any grudge, as Germany may again need Turks to serve their production needs. The rich, the sophisticated, and the educated from Istanbul invariably prefer to go to Germany for a holiday. The Germans also come to Istanbul for a vacation.

The Mercedes cars have endeared themselves in the hearts of the Turks. Turks marry German girls when they can. There is a German hospital in Istanbul, and the German technology is highly respected. The German language has many admirers in Turkey. Germany, also a member of the EEC, is a far closer neighbor than some others in Europe. Germany's prosperity radiates confidence.

Switzerland

Switzerland has been a good friend of Turkey and stands ready to help in every possible way, but the way must be the Swiss way. Switzerland is, therefore, like a frontier of courtesy for Turkey. The banks of Switzerland are ready to help Turkey even when others help no more. SwissAir serviced the Turkish Airlines for quite some time. Turkey produces, in collaboration with Switzerland, certain essential pharmaceutical products.

In 1926 the Swiss Code of Civil Law was adopted by Turkey, largely unchanged. Through the Montreux Convention of 1936, Turkey was able to obtain a revision of the Straits Convention and gain a satisfactory solution of the Alexandretta Dispute through an agreement with France in 1939. It was the Treaty of Lausanne in 1923 which established the present boundaries of Turkey except for the disputed region of Alexandretta (which was acquired by Turkey in 1939). Turkey was to exercise full sovereign rights over its entire territory except the zone of the Straits, which was to remain demilitarized (this last restriction was lifted in 1936).

Italy

The Italians run a hospital in Istanbul. The shipping lines between Italy and Istanbul are effective all the time, and Italy is another member of the EEC. Fiats, made in joint collaboration at a place near Istanbul, flood the streets. The Italian Code of Criminal Law has rule in Turkey since its adoption in 1926 (largely unchanged).

England

The political frontiers between Turkey and England have existed for a long time and even go back to countries which were not then what they are today. It would seem that England usually followed where Turkey had gone before and, when the showdown occurred, the disputed territory usually became first a

British mandate of some kind, which eventually led to freedom of the area or the country concerned, freedom from both the mandate holder and the earlier conqueror. Egypt, Iraq, Palestine, and Cyprus are those with whom Turkey also has had association of conquest, rule, and misrule.

There have also been other types of relationships between England and Turkey which carry the mark of the diplomacy and other skills of England as evolved, exhibited, and performed over many years of activities in Asia, the Middle East, and that part of Europe with which Turkey has been face to face.

When Turkey was the "Sick Man of Europe," during the days of the Ottoman Empire, and later, while wars of conquests and independence went on in the Mideast and Europe in the period of World War I and World War II, in the times of the League of Nations and its successors, with CENTO and without it, as a part of NATO, and now also a member of the EEC, England has always been actively concerned with the "problem of maintaining stability" in the area of which Turkey stands in the middle. That is, England has always shown an everlasting interest in the stability and the future of Turkey.

Yugoslavia

In Yugoslavia, 250,000 people speak Turkish. Yugoslavia is a neighbor of Bulgaria. The Turks and their trucks have to pass through Yugoslavia to go to Europe, just as the Yugoslavs have to pass through Turkey on their eastward business. Yugoslavia belongs to the nonaligned group of nations.

Cyprus

Cyprus is some forty miles south of Turkey in Asia. After A.D. 395 Cyprus was ruled by the Byzantines until 1192. From 1571 Cyprus belonged to the Turks until, in 1878 at the Congress of Berlin, Turkey surrendered its administration to Britain, which annexed it in 1914 and then in 1925 made it a colony of Britain. Negotiations between the British, the Greek, and the Turkish governments in 1960 led to the establishment of an independent Republic of Cyprus (admitted to the British Commonwealth in 1961).

On July 20, 1974, Turkish troops invaded Cyprus following a Greek-oriented coup there. They gained control of important parts of the island. While the Turks were a minority of 17½ percent (the rest were Greek-Cypriots), they, after the invasion of 1974, now occupy 40 percent of the territory of Cyprus.

There are Cypriot-Turks in Turkey, too. Thus, Cypriot-Turks speaking Turkish in Cyprus (more than 110,000 persons in Cyprus speak Turkish) and Turkish-Cypriots speaking Turkish in Turkey between them feel that Cyprus is more Turkish than Greek and, if it cannot all be their own, it should at least continue to be 40 percent Turkish. This is where the matter rests until final decisions can be taken—political, economic, and military decisions.

Israel

Palestine formed part of the Byzantine Empire until A.D. 636, when it was conquered by the Arabs. The Turks conquered the land in 1516 and held it until World War I, when the British conquered it in 1917–18. In 1922, Britain received a mandate from the League of Nations to administer the area, and some 300,000 Jewish emigrants were allowed to enter Palestine during 1920–39. In 1947, Britain announced its intention to give up the mandate on May 15, 1948. Eight hours before the mandate ended, on May 14, 1948, the Jewish agency broadcast a proclamation of a Jewish State of Israel.

Turkish is spoken in Israel, to a limited extent. And whenever an opportunity occurs or can be created, Israel is always waiting and willing to join effort with Turkey, even if it be no more than a matter of a seminar or a project concerned with animals.

At present, Jews (and Druses) constitute a wealthy and effective minority in Turkey, living and flourishing mostly in Istanbul. The links with Israel continue to grow and to prosper, though the relations between Turkey and others on the Arab side of the conflict-war-situation-negotiations also continue to grow and to prosper.

Egypt

Turkey conquered Egypt in 1517, and the conquerors ruled Egypt for two centuries thereafter; then the ruling Turkish pashas could rule no more, having lost control to the Mamelukes, the traditional military aristocracy of Egypt of those days. On the outbreak of World War I in 1914, nominal Turkish sovereignty was abolished and Egypt was declared a British Protectorate.

Egypt is known for many things and the Turks know Egypt more than others, having been one with them as well as their conquerors. While you will not find Egyptian mummies in Istanbul, you will find, instead, Egyptian spices, though Egypt is not known as the international center for spices. You will find these at the Egyptian Bazaar in Istanbul. You must see this bazaar and patronize it, because it is the only one for the exclusive use of Egyptians, their followers, the Turks who went to Egypt, and the Egyptian Turks, and above all for the eaters of spices.

Egypt is now a frontier of courtesy.

Lebanon

Before World War I, Lebanon was part of the Ottoman Empire. In 1922 Lebanon was placed under French mandate. It is estimated that between Syria and Lebanon there are about 210,000 Armenians. Turkey too has Armenians, 70,000 of them, and has had a great deal to do with them in earlier times.

There are several Turks in Lebanon who do good business in

that country. Likewise, there are several Lebanese in Istanbul who not only speak Turkish but also do good business in various fields. The links between Turkey and Lebanon are, however, wider than these facts would seem to suggest.

Afghanistan

Islam is the official religion of Afghanistan and Afghanistan is neighbor of a neighbor and, therefore, between the people of Turkey and the people of Afghanistan there is affinity and regard. In the Turkish market one would find even today carpets from Afghanistan, though naturally old ones, very old ones, brought by travelers or overlords on horseback.

European Economic Community

Since 1964 Turkey has been an associate member of the European Economic Community, the only representative from the Asian part of the world. Turkey is also one of the founder members of the Organization for Economic Cooperation and Development (OECD). The EEC/OECD is, therefore, one of the most cherished extended frontiers of Turkey.

North Atlantic Treaty Organization

As I had some American neighbors who were working in Istanbul as a part of NATO and as I knew some more at Ankara, it might be useful to say a little bit about NATO. After all, Turkey and NATO still stand together, though the Turks keep on showing in their unique, inimitable way that they know best, even with friends and among friends, how to stand aloof and apart.

However, as the U.S.A.-NATO-Turkey situation is subject to change, only a little needs to be said. Having followed a policy of firm alignment with the West for some time, and the Turkish troops having fought in the Korean War, in 1952 Turkey became a full member of the North Atlantic Treaty Organization, and the Turkish (and Greek) forces were integrated in the Southeast European NATO forces. The headquarters of the Sixth Technical Force of NATO was based in Turkey.

Istanbul and Turkey benefited by the prosperity that the NATO relationship brought in. This became all the more apparent when the U.S.A. presence (NATO situation) thinned out after the conflict in Cyprus.

Central Treaty Organization

Turkey concluded a Defense Pact with Yugoslavia and Greece (the Balkan Pact) in 1954 and played a leading part in the creation (1954–55) of the Central Treaty Organization (CENTO). In 1955 a treaty was signed between Turkey and Iraq. Later, in view of the importance of the treaty and the importance of Turkey, Britain, Pakistan, and Iran also joined. In 1958, however, Iraq withdrew from the treaty after the revolution of 1958 in that country. One year later, in 1959, the remaining Allies renamed themselves the Central Treaty Organization, that is, CENTO. So Turkey no longer had a treaty with Iraq, but the alliance continued between Turkey and its frontier and extended frontier allies. However, since 1977 there is no CENTO thriving anywhere.

Alliance of Faith

There are about 700 million followers of Islam throughout the world, with a majority of persons in fifty-seven nations being Muslims. According to another source, the number of Muslims is 430 million, of whom 12 million are in Europe, 320 million in Asia, and 88 million in Africa.

Islam is the principal religion of northwest China, Indonesia, Malaysia, Pakistan, Bangladesh, Afghanistan, Iraq, Syria, Jordan, and the Arabian states as well as part of the Philippines and

Southeast Asia and much of Asian U.S.S.R. It is the religion pre-vailing in Egypt and in the rest of North Africa except Ethiopia. It is also well established in Central Africa and along the eastern coast.

As regards some of the immediate neighbors of Turkey, Islam is the official religion of Iran, and 98 percent of the population of Iran are Muslims. Most of the population of Iraq is Muslim. In Syria, 75 percent of the country's inhabitants are Muslim. Islam is an active religion in that part of the world to which Turkey belongs, and the Islamic brotherhood is extensive and deep. In this brotherhood there are many expectations, and these extend far beyond the secular role of the Republic of Turkey. That is why some call the brotherhood an Alliance of Faith.

As Islam reaches Turkey and begins traveling westward, it begins to taper off and ceases to be practiced as soon as you cross the frontiers on leaving Istanbul. The Belt of Religion, which goes on and on to the East, comes to an end at Istanbul. The position of Turkey in the sphere of Islam is, therefore, most important. Having lasted so long and having gone so far out, when it came to Turkey the state, it was said, in order to break away from backwardness, gave up Islam as its religion and left Islam to the care of its people. Turkey, therefore, in a manner of speaking becomes the terminal point as far as Islam is concerned. And yet, through its people it is as much a part of Islamic world as any other Islamic country.

Turkey is the only country that is a part of the Islamic Brotherhood and yet a founder member of the OECD and an associate member of the EEC. In the case of the other members of the EEC, different forms of Christianity are generally prac-ticed, whereas in the case of Turkey the only worship that is almost universally practiced is Islam.

Turkey is in a position to look at Western friends with desire and even envy. Turkey is also in a position to look at the Islamic Brotherhood with desire and hope. Both these ways of looking are an essential part of the Turkish way of life. So, Turkey when leaning westward is a country steadfast in its relations with the Western allies, and when leaning eastward Turkey is also a country steadfast in its relations with the countries of the Islamic Brotherhood.

Kurds

Southeast Asian Turkey includes parts of Kurdistan, and 6 percent of the population of Turkey speaks Kurdish. The region was held by the Seljuk Turks in the eleventh century and then again after the fifteenth century by the Ottoman Empire. Having struggled for centuries to free themselves from Ottoman rule, the Kurds were granted an autonomous state by the Treaty of Sèvres in 1920, which liquidated the Ottoman Empire. However, the Treaty of Lausanne in 1923, which superseded Sèvres, failed to mention Kurdistan. Revolts by the Kurds of Turkey in 1925 and in 1930 were forcibly quelled by Turkey.

Iran, Turkey, and Iraq have Kurds among them. Turkey has 4 million Kurds, which makes them Turkey's largest minority group. In addition, there are 2 million Kurds in Iraq and another 2 million in Iran. Syria has also about 250,000 Kurds.

The Kurds are all devout Muslims. They keep so much to themselves that you will not meet them in Istanbul (they dwell near the Iranian frontier), but when you do meet them, you will find that they would like to become independent, free from Turkey and free from Iraq and Iran to form a state of their own. The Kurds of Iraq revolted in 1961–70 and obtained recognition of two nationalities in Iraq—Arab and Kurdish—and recognition of the creation of an autonomous Kurdish area.

Armenians

By the Treaty of Sèvres in 1920, Armenia became a separate republic, free from the Ottomans, under international guarantees. Armenia is now one of the republics of the U.S.S.R., and the people of this republic live, border to border, with Turkey on its land frontier with the U.S.S.R.

The total number of Armenian-speakers in the world has been estimated (as of 1974) at 4 million; about 1.5 million live in Soviet Asia, 50,000 in Turkey, 210,000 in Syria and Lebanon, and others in Persia, Iraq, and elsewhere. Some 100,000 emigrated to the U.S.A. According to another estimate, Syria has about 130,000 Armenians and Turkey has 70,000.

If there are now only 70,000 Armenians in Turkey and most of them in Istanbul, you should also know why there are not many more. It is stated that, leaving aside the distant past, there were massacres of Armenians by Turkish troops in 1895, again in 1909, and in 1915, the Turks massacred altogether more than a million Armenians and deported others into the North Syrian desert where they died of starvation. Those who could fled to Russia or Persia, and only some 100,000 were left in Turkish Armenia. It is further stated that those killed and dispersed (more killed than dispersed) during World War I were so massacred and dispersed by the Turks for fear of their collaboration with the U.S.S.R.

65. Empires

THE TURKS HAVE BEEN THE MOST FAMOUS empire builders in the world. Who else? Leaving aside the aspirants and those not so famous or lasting or those far away or, again, those who do not make up even the extended frontiers of Turkey, who are they? The Greeks, the Romans, the Spanish, the Russians, the British, the French, the Persians, and, of course, the Turks.

These facts of glory, conquest, and success need not be mentioned because they are taught in schools and every Turkish boy and girl knows them by heart (and this is the heart of the nationalism of Turkey) and can be expected to recite them word for word. As this continues to be the state of mind, it is good to know these facts when dealing with the present, because the call of the past is also always present.

Some empires may have lasted longer and some have not lasted as long, but the Ottoman Empire of the Turks was famous for over six hundred years. That is, the Turks have been empire builders for six hundred years.

In the fourteenth century B.C., the Hittite Empire in Asia Minor rivaled Babylonia and Egypt. There is an extraordinary and precious Hittite Museum at Ankara for all to see. History also records that the Hittites (1900–1460 B.C.) built the City of Hattwsas (now Bogazkoy) in Eastern Turkey.

From the fourth to the eleventh centuries A.D. the Byzantine Empire dominated. Three centuries later the Turkish-Ottoman Empire began its sweep. The Ottoman Empire was founded in the late thirteenth century and continued until its dissolution in 1918. Modern Turkey formed only a part of this empire, but "Turkey" and the "Ottoman Empire" have often been regarded as one and the same. While the Ottoman Empire began its expansion as early as 1326, the Turkish expansion was at its height in the sixteenth century. In 1541, the major part of Hungary was a part of the Turkish Empire. The Empire moved deep into Persia, Egypt, and Syria, and in 1517 Cairo was a part of it. Only a year later, in 1518, Algiers was taken. Venetian and Latin possessions in Greece also became a part of the Turkish Empire. At one time Vienna was surrounded. There was Turkish domination over the northern part of Africa. The Ottoman Turks controlled the Balkan Peninsula for a long time. And, in spite of the great eastward expansion of Russia in the sixteenth and seventeenth centuries, the shores of the Black Sea were still in the hands of the Ottomans.

When put in another way, it can be said that, having overrun Asia Minor, they began the European conquests by seizing Gallipoli, capturing Constantinople, and becoming masters of the Balkans. They conquered Egypt, Syria, Arabia, Mesopotamia, Tripoli, and most of Hungary. Subsequently, Cyprus was also taken and Crete, too. Later, Russia ousted them from Moldavia, Wallachia, and the Crimea. Still later, Turkey lost Bulgaria, Bosnia, and Herzegovina.

The past shows, undeniably, that the Turks have been the masters of several countries, lands, territories, and zones. Their rule overseas was substantial. When retreating, the Turks left behind their footprints. What they carried forward was their glory. The best of the past has left its mark on the contours of the Turkish psyche and its imprints on the landmarks of the republic.

66. Generalizations and Comparisons

I WILL AVOID COMPARISONS between the Turks and others because, although I lived with the Turks, I have not lived with others for a comparable length of time or as closely as I did with the Turks, and it is difficult to see as fully and as objectively as one should before attempting to make comparisons and draw conclusions. Although I have not made any comparisons, you will be able to make some yourself, depending upon who you are and what your objectives and interests are. I thus leave the Turks in your hands for this limited purpose.

I will also not make generalizations, except in the selected cases in which I feel that a generalization is necessary, justified, and objective and has a purpose to serve (to focus the lens, if you are taking a picture, is essential; to spotlight, if you want the stage and the actors to be seen); to record for future reference as a fact of great common value would also seem justified. Thus, these generalizations will strike you as assessment of relevant facts and of episodes and life stories which have a bearing on my judgments. While some parts of a Turk may be compared with other Turks or even with some parts of those who are not Turks, the Turkish psyche is not to be compared as a whole with the others, and what really matters is the totality. So let the Turk and the Turkish psyche stand by themselves. The following themes will acquaint you with the attitudes of the Turk, especially the Turk in Istanbul.

Be Proud

Be proud—all the time, everywhere, whoever you are, whatever happens, alone and in company, when young, when old, whether unemployed or on top of the world, educated or illiterate. Even when on the run, be proud, all the more when in the wrong. When ahead, show it. When down, bypass it. But be proud. Then you will be yourself and at your best.

You will see this constantly on the national scene. It is the national motto and also the national practice laid down by the Turkish leadership for the Turkish way of life. The first time I saw this was on a banner hung at a meeting of some quality and importance.

Kemal Ataturk said, "Be Proud." So it is.

He also said, "Turks resemble themselves." So be it.

Turkey for Turks

A Turk is proud of his country. He is proud of himself. A Turk is a true nationalist. You should never ever say a word, do a deed, or think a thought which does not add luster, honor, and glory to Turkey and her great and noble sons.

Should you, however, ever find yourself in the most unlikely and unfortunate situation in which a Turk says something about himself or his government or anything at all about Turkey which does not reflect well on the subject under contemplation, never under any circumstances whatsover lend your ear. Hear but hear not. See but see not. Do not agree with him. Do not aid or abet him in his comment or criticism. By your total withdrawal allow him also to withdraw himself totally from what he might have said. You are then his best friend.

Style

The Turkish way of life is completely independent of any alien style, and you must never confuse it with external styles, such as style of painting, decoration, appearance, performance, driving, singing, smoking, drinking, writing, discussion, negotiation. Style by its nature means something that will change with the times, and some new style is being created every day. It, in the end, means doing what others are doing (the Turks do not like to follow) or setting the pace for others to follow (the Turks know that others will not follow them).

In the case of the Turk, however, it is always important to stand erect, alone, aloof, and upright. The Turkish way of life, therefore, has no room or time for style. However, if you persist you will surely find a confusion of different styles. This is because if there were only one particular style, even at a given point of time, it might interfere with what is basic in Turkey.

If your persistence goes still deeper, you will also find that apart from confusion there is also conflict. The Turks, while they have no complexes, do suffer from conflicts, though these have no lasting or disturbing effect. The conflict is because some Turks, who wish to appear better off than other Turks, would like to adopt, at least for superficial reasons, styles prevalent elsewhere. Others who have no such ambition look down upon such adoptions and adaptations. This creates a conflict.

Sometimes, the highly sophisticated and the richest do find the Western style somewhat acceptable, but that is because this particular style, in their opinion, only underscores the qualities of the Turkish way of life. The Turkish way of life is the only permanent and unique way of life.

To and Fro

An interesting example of the Turk who always stands erect and upright became apparent on one particular occasion which concerned the PLO and Israel. The PLO expected that there would be a PLO Office in Turkey set up with the approval and support of the government, which had expressed warm sympathies for the PLO. But this did not happen. Israel expected that Turkey would go all the Israeli way. But this too did not happen. Turkey does not belong to the group of nonaligned countries, as is well known. This is not necessary in the case of Turkey; Turkey knows how to stand erect and upright. The maximum that may happen from time to time is that an individual, when angry or upset, may lean forward and then lean backward until he may lean no more and gets back to his standing position, erect and upright.

Don't Laugh

Don't laugh at the Turks. Not even at a single Turk, if friendship is what holds the two of you together. Nobody likes to be laughed at. But the reason in the case of the Turks is deeper. No Turk ever laughs at himself. Not even at another Turk. That being the case, you do not dare to laugh at any one of them!

It is not only a matter of laughing at them. Even if it means to laugh with them, don't do it. (In any case, you will have to wait a long time for such an opportunity to arise.) When there are more amiable ways, when there are also serious matters to attend to, when the mind is fully taken up with state and social affairs, where is the time to laugh, anyway? And who said that humor and laughter are essential? All that matters is the Turkish way of life.

Courtesy

The Turks in Istanbul were always extremely polite and courteous to each other, alone or together. They were also, without fail, equally polite and courteous even if you were not a Turk. Istanbul is one of the most polite cities in the world.

But from time to time it is only natural that an argument would become hot and, when heated, people behave differently. In Istanbul two aspects of such a situation were almost always true: no one else joined in the fray; and as the heat increased and the argument developed, each one would sway, forward-backward, backward-forward, without shuffling feet or body touching body. The thrashing of hands and the beating of breasts only lent color to the quarrel. But at its peak, the quarrel was no more than a threat, and the legal threat was the highest in the armory of the argument.

Turkish Face

The Turks are very handsome, both women and men. With their origin and birth, with their attitude of mind and their seven months of sunshine and swimming, with their bread, fruit, and cheese, milk and butter, the rich, the educated, and the sophisticated in Istanbul are very beautiful indeed. And all beauty is in the face.

The Mask

Beauty requires care, and the more beautiful the face the greater care it needs. Creams, lotions, powder, and paint are for outward beauty, but for inner beauty—physical, mental, spiritual, and emotional—more is needed. What is required is a mask. The mask must be comprehensive, effective, and made to order to fit each face and to suit various circumstances as these arise from time to time.

Usually the mask consists of pride (this could become arrogance from time to time), poise, self-confidence, eternal faith to one's self always being in the right (never ever being in the wrong, admitting to any wrongdoing, or doing any wrong of any kind whatsoever), self-reliance, courage, living in the present, and being strong in one's head.

Another layer in the makeup of the mask consists of always knowing every possible way and direction, polite and courteous, relaxed, intolerant of others' cultures, hard-working, untiring, always awake, difficult to probe, asking less and less, retreating from others' questions. The further layers consist of obedience to parents and other agents of authority, being selective of words and deeds, holding hands with each other against alien hands, never being off guard, never complaining or blaming, and admitting nothing. Still others consist of being hospitable, protective of morals, guardian of property, asking Allah for nothing, showing off in big ways, being indifferent to change and aware only of the best of the days gone by, always on the path of glory, valor, conquest, and honor.

The mask is as essential to the beauty of the face as beauty is to the face of the Turk.

Freedoms

The Turks enjoy all freedoms: freedom from state religion; freedom from disease and ill-health; freedom to work; freedom from each other; freedom from want (even when poor); freedom of speech (and silence too); freedom from company (erect, aloof, and upright); freedom of choice; freedom from illusions; freedom from danger; freedom from the failures of the past; freedom of free thought and philosophy; freedom from mental burdens; freedom to be on one's own; freedom from requests and obligations; freedom from compulsions and complexes and fears and expectations.

The Turk is a completely free spirit, and in his own free way he is also free from what lies ahead and what the future will do or not do for him. He is so free that he is engaged in the display of life as it is lived always in the present, "the instant made eternity." In the time capsule, the present is the continuation of the past at its very best (the only past that matters) and instead of living buried underneath, he lives above the level of ground. There is, however, one freedom which he does not enjoy fully, that is, the freedom from the total entirety of the past. Here his freedom is partial and circumscribed.

Try and compare these freedoms with yours and you will realize what deep cuts have been made into yours, and which ones have rusted most, and how far your own freedoms have now become only rights to be secured through the long-cherished legal system, and how little you can do alone and on your own!

Bounties

Both nature and man are kind to the Turk, kindest of all to the Turk in Istanbul. When earthquakes occur, they occur far away. Poverty, the creation of man, is not as bad as it could be and is in other places. Istanbul has peace on its borders, and Turkey looks after Istanbul above everything else. The minorities live in safety, prosperity, and happiness. Different races and colors and religions mix well in Istanbul. When cholera occurs (smallpox does not), it is merely a scare. The media do not oppress the citizens of Istanbul.

The variety that exists in Istanbul, the changes that occur, and the people that come and go all lend charm to life in Istanbul. In Istanbul the upper echelons live in their own civilized ways. The Kurds and the problems they create from time to time are not the concern of Istanbul. The taxes are not heavy. The sources and the centers of power are many. The law that govern the city are comprehensive and well administered.

Istanbul is independent of what goes on elsewhere in Turkey.

The system works in Istanbul. There is no religious or any other impediment. Property is well protected. If the city is old, it is young too. It is growing like an adolescent and in many ways it is another Eternal City. You can get all the education you want in Istanbul. You can come and go as you like into other parts of Turkey, and you can also go outside into the wide world as you wish. If you are not too close to the extremes of Turkey, you are not too far either. The language is no barrier nor any social custom or tradition. Which tribe is your own is your own business in every way. There is no conscription, and when the Turk does military duty he is just being trained for national service.

Foreigners like to do business in Istanbul. No pleasure is denied to them and all are within reach. You can live where you like in Istanbul without authorization. You can live elsewhere too, if you like. There is no monsoon, no drought, no tigers, no head hunters, no marauders, no predators, no forest fires, no floods, no hurricanes, no typhoons, no tempests, no avalanches, no body snatchers, no one at all to do you any harm or to cause you any inconvenience or interference. You are also not an isolated island but you have islands around you for your pleasure. No one dare step on your toes.

Fears and Expectations

While the individual Turk may not have any fears or expectations, and while Turkey may not give expression to any fears and may not even be too outspoken about certain expectations, there were others (mostly those who were not directly concerned or involved) who did give expression to fears and expectations. Incidentally, within the country, while there were discussions and debates, seminars and meetings and even memoranda sent to the government indicative of what was not right or what was wrong and even what should be done, these could not be called an expression of fears and expectations.

The fears that the outsider had were about the position of Turkey in the outside world, about the foreign-currency situation, about the extent of industrialization of the country, the extent of military preparedness, about its reliability in the hour of need, about its relations with the Arabs and other Islamic countries, about its being almost lonely and alone from time to time, about its reliance on Europe, its dependence on the U.S.A., the U.S.S.R., and some other neighbors.

Seldom did these outsiders bother to refer to fears about the situation within the country, about the persistent inequalities, the position of rural areas, unemployment, social instability, and other matters such as these. Mention came to be made about the internal situation from time to time, but that was more in respect of the political situation and the instability or lack of government, and that too because it affected the position of Turkey in the outside world.

The real expectations were the unexpressed ones of the people themselves, which seldom reached the surface. These related to sharing gains of prosperity, better law and order, better health and education, freedom from bureaucracy, more employment, and other day-to-day matters which generally concern the common man. The unexpressed fears were also of the same type. The common man was getting more and more left behind.

It is, therefore, necessary to state clearly what the true compulsions and what the true imperatives are and why a great deal must be done about them, and done without delay.

Imperatives

There are certain imperatives for Turkey and to put these in the sharpest possible form, they deserve to be arranged as follows:

1. The need to shed some centuries
2. True involvement of the people in all affairs of society and state

3. Self-containment
4. Collaboration with others
5. To move with the times so as to be ahead of the times
6. Realization of reality
7. Political understanding and accommodations even if it be not stability at all levels
8. Preservation of rights and enforcement of responsibilities
9. The widest possible dispersal of wealth
10. Rural development and land reform on the largest possible scale
11. More employment for youth
12. Higher levels of skills
13. Improvement in standards of education
14. Total equality for its citizens, for the minorities, and for all who have made Turkey their own country

Compulsions

Certain inevitable, powerful compulsions, too, must be reckoned with, for instance:

1. Time is running out
2. The inevitable will not accommodate anyone
3. Progress and development do not follow accelerated paths, year by year
4. The art of rapid development is still being developed and has not yet been fully mastered
5. The stakes are high
6. Social change must be universal
7. Dispersal of wealth does not happen by itself

Compulsions such as these and many more affect a large number of countries, and Turkey and its people are no exception. How effectively these are dealt with and within what time limits and on what scale will largely determine the retention of the existing bounties and the further gains that can be obtained in the years ahead.

Turkey has had a great past, a present which is both shining and dull, depending upon where you stand, and Turkey will have, so far as forecasts go, an everlasting future. It is now up to the Turks!

INDEX

Index